JUDICIAL POLITICS IN THE OLD REGIME

Judicial Politics
in the Old Regime

THE PARLEMENT OF PARIS DURING THE REGENCY

James D. Hardy, Jr.

LOUISIANA STATE UNIVERSITY PRESS
BATON ROUGE

For my wife,
whose love made this book possible

Copyright © 1967 by
Louisiana State University Press

Library of Congress Catalog Card Number: 67-21375

Manufactured in the United States of America by
The Seeman Printery, Inc., Durham, North Carolina

Designed by Jules B. McKee

PREFACE

AT THE BEGINNING of the Regency the Parlement of Paris emerged from a long political decline. Defeated in the Fronde of 1648, the Parlement had been systematically excluded by Louis XIV from the exercise of its traditional political powers. After likening itself to a Senate, the Parlement was reduced to a bench, concerned only with the administration of laws and the passing of judgments. Louis XIV never ceased to consider the Parlement an enemy.

There were sound reasons for such judgment both in the *Grand Siècle* and later in the Regency. For the Parlement of Paris, and the other sovereign courts as well, were enemies of the crown's persistent policy of centralizing political power and undermining local, feudal, and provincial privileges. The Parlement, however, had not always opposed the crown in its attempts to create a bureaucratic, centralized monarchy. Philip the Fair had used the Parlement to condemn Edward I of England as a contumacious vassal. Charles V had used it to increase his tax collection. Charles VII had found the Parlement a useful weapon against local vassals. Francis I had the Parlement annul the Treaty of Madrid. But in the seventeenth century the kings of France and their ministers centralized through intendants and royal councils rather than through their court system. A new bureaucracy,

v

built around the King's ministers and their departments, replaced the courts as the instruments of increasing royal power. The Parlements, once composed of the King's men, now changed, until by the Fronde they became the eloquent defenders of ancient privilege, entrenched local rights, and provincial autonomy. They upheld the diversities of medieval France and opposed the King in his drive toward centralization, toward a systematic, rational government, toward "absolutism."

The Parlements were still, of course, part of the royal government. They registered and disseminated the King's edicts, enforced his laws, received his attorneys, and tried his cases. Even in eclipse under Louis XIV they conducted a great part of the King's administration. But the Parlements were no longer in accord with the King's policies. Throughout the entire eighteenth century France witnessed the spectacle of the major judicial body of the realm consistently opposing important royal legislation. On questions of financial policy, of royal prerogatives and rights, and of the Gallican liberties, the King and his Parlement were irrevocably divided. On these issues the judiciary conducted a permanent cold war against the executive and legislative power vested in the King. This divided government went on and on, from John Law through the abortive tax reform in 1749, to the Jesuits in the 1760's and the constitutional quarrel in the 1770's, and ended only with the Estates-General in 1788 and 1789. The Regency set the pattern for a prolonged civil war at the very heart of the French government. Judicial politics, an important element in the medieval centralization of the French monarchy, was no mean factor in the coming of a revolution which destroyed that monarchy.

This study seeks to clarify both the general patterns

and the necessary details of the Parlement's judicial politics at its inception, during the Regency. The issues of financial policy, the Gallican liberties, and the constitutional position of the Parlement were raised then. The techniques of protest and repression and of appeal to public opinion were inaugurated during the Regency. The moral and political positions of both the Parlement and the King were established in the financial and religious conflicts which occurred between 1715 and 1723. John Law and the exile to Pontoise were the prototypes of a political drama which ended only with revolution. During the Regency the royal government was quite strong and put the Parlement in its place rather easily. Later ministries would find this a much harder task. But the patterns of political confrontation remained stable, while the results of these conflicts turned steadily in the Parlement's favor as the Revolution neared. The crown grew less resolute and the magistrates bolder. From the 1750's on, the Parlement was frequently victorious. The Parlement's judicial politics during the Regency set the pattern for the conflicts, though not their results, for the rest of the Old Regime.

Thanks for this book must be rendered first to Dr. Otakar Odlozilik of the University of Pennsylvania. A sympathetic teacher and a brilliant scholar, he guided the work from its beginning. Professor A. J. Slavin of UCLA was most generous with his time and criticism. The Samuel Fels Foundation of Philadelphia supplied the grant which enabled me to go to France to do the archival research which led to this book. And finally there is Professor Edward W. Fox of Cornell University, whose generous support through the years is gratefully acknowledged.

J. D. H., JR.

Baton Rouge

CONTENTS

JUDICIAL POLITICS IN THE OLD REGIME

CHAPTER I

1715

AT EIGHT-FIFTEEN on the morning of September 1, 1715, Louis XIV died. The Duke of Bouillon, Grand Chamberlain of France, wearing a black plume in his hat, appeared on the balcony of the King's chamber and cried out, "The King is dead!" He went back in, reappeared a moment later with a white plume, and cried three times, "Long live King Louis XV!"[1] An era had ended. The Regency had begun.

Louis XIV had reigned and ruled for seventy-two years. Few Frenchmen had lived under another King, and almost none could remember one. All French life bore the impact of the measured majesty of the Sun King, but no aspect more so than politics. Louis XIV had abased the great and turned them into idle courtiers, reduced the sovereign courts to impotence, gained control over the administration and the army, and placed the throne above contending factions. Politics and administration functioned at his command. Throughout the long years of his reign, Louis had endeavored, and with some success, to keep each rank of court and country in an unchanging and exact relationship with every other. A fixed and secure social order, as divinely ordained as the moral, had been his goal. The entire regime presented a facade of changeless and majestic conservatism, a spectacle so impressive

[1] Jean Buvat, *Journal de la Régence*, ed. E. Campardon (Paris, 1865), I, 47.

3

that few seriously hoped for change until the death of the King.

At Versailles and his country estates Louis created a world only remotely connected to the rest of France. He disliked Paris, was hardly there five times in the last twenty years of his reign, and discouraged his courtiers from going. Attendance upon his person and the constant round of activities and amusements he devised became the sole function of a courtier. Exile from his view meant destruction and penury and was the constant nightmare of the great. Those who attended the *grande levée*, or were seen by the King, had their petitions granted. The uninvited or the unrecognized had to wait. The phrase "He is a man I never see" became an inexorable sentence of doom.

"Never was a man so naturally polite, nor with so measured a politeness, nor so polite by degrees, nor one who distinguished better age, merit, rank. . . ." [2] With grave courtesy and colossal devotion to detail, Louis regulated the lives of his courtiers. At his disposal were titles and honor and considerable wealth, which he carefully dispensed to the nobility. His insatiable attention to the minutiae of court etiquette and ritual enabled Louis to extend indefinitely the range and scope of his favors. Because his financial resources alone could never cope with the constant stream of petitions for pensions and advancement, he created, bit by bit, an enormous web of titles, privileges, courtesies, and gradations, and endowed them with a value surpassing life itself. The King did not ignore the precise measure due each person and rank and exacted similar behavior from his courtiers and their ser-

[2] Louis de Rouvroy, Duke of Saint-Simon, *Mémoires*, ed. A. de Boislisle (Paris, 1879–1928), XXVII, 145.

vants. Never was a man of lower estate given the honors due a peer. For a country gentleman the King merely lifted his hat; for a marquis he raised it; for ladies or a prince of the blood, he swept it off and bowed. Double doors were opened only for the King's immediate family; for the rest, just one side.

Gradations even more meaningless assumed unbelievable proportions. Princesses sat in chairs, duchesses on stools, and the rest stood. Guests invited to Marly, the King's favorite retreat, were considered the cream of the court, holding the monarch's special favor. Yet even they were divided. On the doors of some merely the name was chalked. But for other, happier courtiers, the phrase "Pour le . . . de . . ." appeared. Obtaining *les pours* meant extraordinary favor, and produced, as if by magic, swarms of clients and place seekers. On each visit the King changed *les pours* from one to another, and each had his moment. As a result, the King centered on his person an honorific ladder of prestige and rank, a hierarchy of minute court distinctions.

At Versailles these things were reality. But outside, away from the Sun King, such honors as *les pours* had little meaning. So except for war the courtiers seldom ventured far from Versailles and the King, and slowly forgot that there was any other France. For a while France did not forget them. Particularly in Paris, news and gossip of the court were eagerly exchanged, and the courtiers' functions were considered exceptionally vital. But this did not endure. As the great edifice of Versailles neared completion, the interest of the country in its inhabitants began to wane. Boredom and outright hostility replaced admiration. Intellectual life in the last two decades of the Sun King's reign moved from the royal court to Paris. At the very time when the tribal customs of Versailles were becoming most rigid and complex, they began to matter less and less, and the France beyond Versailles began to count for more and more.

Over twenty million people lived in the world beyond Versailles. Most of these were peasants, noticed by the King only when they refused to pay their taxes or revolted. For these the years from 1690 to 1712, the period of the League of Augsburg and the War of the Spanish Succession, were a time of famine, the worst of the eighteenth century. The nadir was reached in 1709. The turn of the year brought disaster; the months of January and February were a continual siege of dank and bitter cold. Birds and animals were found dead by the roadside, and unfortunate travelers dropped beside them. Rivers froze over and carried the weight of heavy wagons. As the cold continued week on week, the poor and least protected began to die. As far south as Languedoc, wolves were reported in the fields and even in the villages. Near Paris, Madame de Maintenon reported, 24,000 people died from the cold in January alone. And the spring was no better. After an early thaw the cold came back, killing the fruit trees, vines, and early sowing. A wet summer accompanied by hail storms, military defeat, and continued starvation completed the disaster.

Starvation, endemic to the peasant and urban poor, came early in 1709. There were reports from the Ile de France and Anjou of men eating grass and bark, infallible signs of famine. By March even these were gone. Starving peasants roamed the countryside, killing what game they could find. The little food hoarded in the villages was stolen by gangs of brigands. Over vast areas of France law broke down completely, and towns expelled visitors and shut their gates as in time of siege. Commerce and government were reduced to a trickle. Only army recruiters roamed the villages at will, promising bread to the dying peasant lads if they would enlist.

There was little enough food even for Marshal Villars' ragged army, which stood alone between Paris and the dreaded Englishman Marlborough. Wheaten bread had disappeared even from the tables of Versailles. Black bread, oats, and barley were all that could be found at any price. In Paris the price of the worst bread rose ten times during the year, and flour was moved under troop convoy. Toulouse, center of one of the richest areas of France, suffered repeated bread riots in the spring and summer of 1709. The wrath of God lay heavy on the land, and a bitter litany was heard.

Our Father, who art at Marly, thy name is no longer hallowed; thy Kingdom is no longer so great; thy will is no longer done on earth or on the waters. Give us our bread, which on every side we lack. Forgive our enemies, who have beaten us, and not our generals who have allowed them to do so. Do not succumb to the temptations of Maintenon, but deliver us from Chamillart.[3]

Deliver us from cold, hunger, war, and disaster. Louis was not God, but he did what he could. He acted better in adversity than he ever did in triumph. He nullified the taxes of the poor and appealed to the rich. He sent his New Year's gift to the treasury, cut the pensions of his family, sent his plate to the mint, and sold his jewels. But only the return of good weather, the providential victory at Malplaquet, and the desertion of the English from the allied cause saved him. Nothing could revive the pros-

[3] Quoted in Jacques Boulanger, *The Seventeenth Century in France* (Capricorn edition; New York, 1963), 307.

perity and confidence of the "beautiful years." The King
had fallen into discredit, and all levels and ranks waited
for him to die.

The Sun King died slowly. Never for a moment during his last years did he fail to perform his task of governing France. The reins of power remained firmly in his
hands until the very last, and this power, so lately rescued
from the shadow of Marlborough, was not idly or inconsequentially used. If the last years of the Sun King were
barren of achievement, they were crowded with events.
No political decisions were more important than those
which Louis made in the years between 1710 and his
death five years later.

Louis' last years were darkened by an appalling series
of personal disasters. On April 17, 1711, the King's son
and heir to the throne died of smallpox at the château of
Meudun. The King was greatly affected by his loss and
controlled himself with difficulty. This tragedy was followed by others. On February 18, 1712, the new heir, the
Duke of Burgundy, died, presumably of scarlet fever, in
any case of so virulent a fever that the doctors were helpless before it. He had been preceded to the grave by his
wife by six days and was followed by his son, then heir,
the Duke of Brittany, on March 11. All fell under the
same scythe. In a year, and mostly within a single month,
the royal succession, once so full of candidates, was reduced to a sickly child of two, the future Louis XV. The
throne was in danger of passing to collateral lines. Worse
yet, it might be claimed by Philip V of Spain, even though
he had made solemn renunciation, and war with Great
Britain would begin again. No one knew better than the
King that an exhausted France simply could not afford a
succession crisis.

Louis took the measures he considered necessary to insure a peaceful succession. In August, 1714, he had an edict registered in the Parlement of Paris which placed his two illegitimate sons, the Duke of Maine and the Count of Toulouse, in line for the throne after the other princes of the blood.[4] In May, 1715, he raised the two natural princes to the full rank of prince of the blood.[5] Whatever the legal merits of such action were, they did not concern the King. Had the King the right to alter the line of succession, or did such things come from God? Louis cared not at all. France needed peace, and he loved his two natural sons. A King had his duty, and in this case duty was a pleasure. But he was not deceived as to the possible reactions of the Duke of Maine's enemies. One of his last recorded conversations with his son illustrates his profound doubts about the efficacy of this arrangement: "You know that however great I make you, you will be nothing after my death, and it will be your business to turn all that I have done for you to account— if you can."[6] The first act of the Regency would be to see if the Duke of Maine could maintain his position.

Religion as well as succession aggravated the old man's years. Although Jansenism as a doctrinal force had all but died by the first decade of the eighteenth century,

[4] Text of the edict is in M. Isambert and others (eds.), *Recueil général des anciennes lois françaises depuis l'an 420 jusqu'à la Révolution de 1789* (Paris, 1821–33), XX, 619–22. Minutes of the ceremony of registration are in Buvat, *Journal de la Régence*, I, 503–10.

[5] "Déclaration du Roy que le duc du Maine et le comte de Toulouse et leurs descendens en légitime marriage prendront la qualité de prince du sang royal," Bibliothèque Nationale, série F 23621 (77), May 23, 1715. Bibliothèque Nationale is hereinafter cited as B.N. See also Isambert and others (eds.), *Recueil général*, XX 641–42.

[6] Quoted in W. H. Lewis, *Louis XIV: An Informal Portrait* (New York, 1959), 210.

it was still accounted a menace to the discipline of the Church. In 1693 Pasquier Quesnel published his *Réflexions morales sur le Nouveau Testament,* which was immediately branded a new and dangerous compendium of Jansenist error. Even more distressing was the continued defiance of the nuns of Port Royal des Champs. A court order demanded the confiscation of their property, and a papal letter charged them to disperse, but the twenty-two old women continued to resist. From 1707 to 1709 the nuns held the world at bay, assisted by the sympathy of Cardinal Noailles, himself suspected of Jansenism. But on July 2, 1709, the cardinal was forced to order the convent closed, and the nuns dispersed. Amid piteous scenes of leave-taking, the aged and infirm nuns were carted off to exile. Compassion for their plight was general in Paris and greatly strengthened the Jansenist movement.[7] Papal proclamations were no more effective than royal authority, and Jansenist disaffection was to survive the Sun King.

Finances made further demands on the royal attention. The War of the Spanish Succession had drained the treasury. Extraordinary methods of finance were used until they became customary. Taxes were raised. In 1705 two *sous pour livre* surtax was levied on all farmed taxes—*gabelles, aides, traites* and *domaines* alike. Patents of nobility and government offices were sold, revoked, and sold again. Government paper was issued to cover obligations. Huge loans were raised and promptly fell to a fraction of par. Cities bought charters of privileges. Elbeuf in Normandy, for example, used the fiscal crisis to

[7] See Ernest Moret, *Quinze Ans du règne de Louis XIV* (Paris, 1859), III, 317–19.

purchase exemption from the *taille* in 1705.[8] The correspondence of the intendants was filled with gloom and despair and reiterated constantly that the provinces were unable to pay. The end of the war saved France from bankruptcy, but the Sun King was too old, and too preoccupied with his family, to attempt any reform. That could wait for a Regency.

New men, old problems, a new broom; that is what the French expected of the approaching Regency. It would be too much to say that France eagerly awaited the death of Louis XIV. But the nation rejoiced when it came.

I

During the long reign of Louis XIV the Parlement of Paris had seen its political power reduced to nothing and its ancient constitutional pretensions completely ignored. In previous reigns each political setback had been temporary, and the Parlement had managed to evade the restrictions placed upon its conduct. But Louis XIV had decisively informed the magistrates that their duty was obedience. The era of the Sun King, glorious for French arms and literature, was dark indeed for the Parlements of France.

There can be little doubt that the reign of Louis XIV consolidated a constitutional and political change in France which had been long in coming. The medieval monarchy, based on mutually contracted obligations, had nearly disappeared under the blows of the wars of religion, the ministries of Sully, Richelieu, and Mazarin, and the constant fiscal pressure of the crown on its subjects. France may not have been transformed into a modern

[8] See the excellent monograph by Jeffrey Kaplow, *Elbeuf during the Revolutionary Period* (Baltimore, 1964), Chap. 1.

state and society under the Sun King, but the Renaissance monarchy was gone.[9] The crown had obtained by prescriptive right the power to judge and tax far beyond what had been granted by the feudal oath of loyalty. The royal household had been converted into a state independent of individual ministers and nobles, and a bureaucratic nexus had been substituted for a personal one. Much had changed since Henry III.

Constitutional theories changed to reflect the altered political conditions. When the political theorist Jean Bodin wrote of sovereignty, he thought of the powers of the crown rather than of the liberties and immunities of the subjects. A civil lawyer and a participant in the wars of religion, Bodin imagined a rationalized monarchy, freed from the rickety anomalies of feudal privilege. Nor was he alone in so thinking. Cardin Le Bret, advocate-general of the Parlement of Paris and a councilor of state, spread similar theories in an apology for the government of Cardinal Richelieu. His comment that "Kings may use their power to change old ordinances and laws of their states . . . because the King is the only sovereign in his Kingdom, and sovereignty is no more divisible than the point in geometry . . ." did not strike most of his fellow magistrates as a particularly valuable contribution to the continuing discussion of constitutional theory.[10] But Le Bret's statement did reflect political reality. The magistrates of the Regency, however, maintained an ambivalent

[9] See J. R. Major, *Representative Institutions in Renaissance France, 1421–1559* (Madison, 1960); and R. Mousnier and F. Hartung, "Quelques problèmes concernant la monarchie absolue," in *Storia Moderna* (Florence, 1955).

[10] Cardin Le Bret, *Traité de la Souveraineté du Roy, de son Domaine et de sa Couronne* (Paris, 1632), 70–72. For a brief commentary on Le Bret, see Paul Doolin, *The Fronde* (Cambridge, Mass., 1935), Chap. IV.

attitude toward these changes in the royal government. As politicians, they understood that the powers of the crown had been greatly extended. As constitutional lawyers, they refused to admit that anything had changed. The old constitution of their theories, so ancient that no one could tell for certain if it had ever existed, was to be revived *in toto* by the Parlement of 1715. The magistrates, with their archives and theoretical treatises, claimed to understand the proper constitution of France. They would bring it back.

The judges of the Parlements believed in the rule of law. Written or customary, Roman or feudal, the laws of the realm were the fabric of government and justice. Individual laws and customs were at the discretion of the King, but law in general stood above him. The jurist and diplomat Claude de Seyssel expressed the magistrates' belief when he wrote: "The King and Monarch, knowing that by means of Law, Ordinances, and excellent customs of France concerning the Police, the Kingdom has come to such glory, grandeur, and power that it now has, and maintains its peace, prosperity and reputation, ought to guard them and have them observed as much as he is able, considering also that he is obliged to do so by the oath which he takes at his coronation. . . ." [11] Custom could change; fundamental law could not.

The fundamental laws of France, though not a constitution in the modern sense, could be considered the political axioms accepted by the vast majority of the legal and political aristocracy of the land.[12] They were not written

[11] Claude de Seyssel, *La Monarchie de France*, ed. Jacques Poujol (Paris, 1961), II, 154.

[12] For a good discussion of the fundamental laws of France, see André Lemaire, *Les lois fondamentales de la monarchie française d'après les théoriciens de l'ancien régime* (Paris, 1907); and Ralph Giesey, *Juristic Basis of Dynastic Right* (Philadelphia, 1963).

down in a body, and neither their number nor their content was generally agreed upon. Yet all held that they existed, included such things as the Salic law, and were basic to the constitutional workings of the realm. The magistrates of the Parlement were particularly attached to this concept. They were convinced that they knew what the fundamental laws were. Achille de Harlay, a First President of the Parlement of Paris, appealed to the concept of fundamental law in defending his court against Henry III. He observed: "There are two kinds of Law, Sire: one is composed of ordinances of the King which may change according to the time and the necessities; the other includes ordinances of the realm. These last are inviolable and among them is one, the most holy, which our Kings have always observed—never to publish a law or ordinance which has not been verified by this Company." [13] The magistrates not only believed in the existence of the fundamental laws, they held the Parlement to be the guardian of them. With their immense archives the magistrates claimed, and not completely illogically, that they alone knew what the "maxims of the kingdom" were and what precedents existed for any royal edict. The magistrates felt that it was their job to see that these maxims were not broken, that the rights of the King remained intact, and that the liberties of the subjects were not disturbed.

Being guardian of the fundamental laws was a glorious self-conception, but more specific formulation was necessary for it to be politically viable. The magistrates of the Regency were attempting to obtain extensive political

[13] Quoted in the remonstrance of the Parlement of Paris of January 17, 1771. See Jules Flammermont (ed.), *Les Remontrances du Parlement de Paris au XVIIIe siècle* (Paris, 1888–98), III, 178.

powers, stemming as necessary corollaries from their view of the fundamental laws of France. The Parlement claimed untrammelled judicial power within the court's competence and the political rights of registration of edicts, modification of edicts, and remonstrance against what the magistrates thought to be a poor edict. This was an ambitious program and required all the legal justification the magistrates could muster.

For the Parlement, no edict of the crown was valid until it had been registered by the court. Edicts registered by the Parlement, that is, approved and signed by the court, were constitutional and did not contradict the "maxims of the kingdom" or the rights of the King. Thus, they were law. Edicts not so registered were suspect and ought not to be law. No one upheld this view with more vigor than the canon Claude Joly in his defense of the Fronde. He wrote that "Kings are established principally to do justice—I do not think it difficult to prove that they are likewise held to the laws, since that which does not conform to approved laws cannot be held just. . . ." Concerning the particular powers of the Parlement he added: "The laws and ordinances of the King ought to be verified in the Parlement . . . otherwise the subjects are not bound by them. And when the Court adds to the publication 'by the express command of the King,' it indicates the Court has not found the Edict reasonable. . . ." [14] In a remonstrance of 1718 the Parlement was to make this clear to the Regent. The court "dared to say that it is to the interest of Your Majesty's subjects, and even to

[14] Claude Joly, *Recueil des Maximes Véritables et Importantes pour l'Instruction du Roy contre la Pernicieuse Politique du Cardinal Mazarin, Sur-Intendant de l'Education de Sa Majesté* (Paris, 1652, 1663). These passages were translated from the 1663 edition, which was condemned to be burned.

Yourself, that your laws be transmitted to the people by the normal means, which are the registration and publication by the Parlement. . . ." [15] To the magistrates registration was the symbol of both the constitutionality of edicts and the power of the Parlement.

Registration was also politically important. France was not so centralized that royal edicts were exactly and implicitly obeyed everywhere, regardless of the opinions of the local magnates. The willingness of secondary courts and judicial officials to accept royal commands, and their enthusiasm in enforcing them, were major factors in seeing that these edicts were obeyed. The Parlement's registration helped considerably. It meant that the Parlement would probably uphold the edict on judicial appeal. It also meant that the Parlement thought the edict proper and workable, and the local tribunals, to whom the court sent these registered laws, were very likely to reflect this view. Enforcement of registered laws, particularly taxation measures, was much simpler than was that of laws which were not sealed. Even the simple dissemination of the royal will was much aided by the cooperation of the Parlement and the local judicial system. As a practical political measure, registration by the Parlement had much to recommend it to the crown. As such it was a powerful weapon for the court.

Modification of edicts once registered and in force was much the same thing. Not all edicts would prove workable in practice, reasoned the magistrates. The Parlement, therefore, claimed the power to modify judicially an edict which had proved imperfect, to strike out an offending passage, to inject a new meaning into an old phrase.

[15] "Remontrance sur l'affaire de la réfonte des monnaies," June 17, 1718, in Flammermont (eds.), *Les Remontrances*, I, 78.

In addition to this judicial modification, the Parlement claimed the right to change laws during registration. As the crown was unlikely to send deliberately defective and unworkable edicts to the Parlement, it seems clear that the magistrates were asking for a significant share in the royal legislative power. They wanted nothing less than a veto.

The third political demand of the Parlement was the right of making a remonstrance to the King on an edict before registering it. In their remonstrance the magistrates informed the King what they thought was wrong with his edict and why it could not be registered. A remonstrance was a protest, nothing more. Since Louis XIV had taken the right of remonstrance away, however, it had become the symbol of the Parlement's political pretensions. A remonstrance could delay the publication of a law while King and court wrangled over its provisions. Finally, a public dispute could, and often did, raise a formidable tide of public opinion against the King and effectively defeat an offensive edict.

The King could only oppose such constitutional doctrine. Concerning the Parlement, royal absolutism had a program of almost mechanistic simplicity. The King recognized the Parlement as a judicial body existing on sufferance alone. The court was to be dependent on the royal will, function at the King's command, and hold its prerogatives as a reflection of royal glory. Even the judicial functions of the Parlement were at the pleasure of the crown and could be revoked at will. Such doctrine reflected the realities of the immediate past. In 1667, and again in 1673, Louis XIV had reduced the political power of the Parlement and made new procedural arrangements for the administration of justice.[16] He had ordered that edicts sent to the Parlement be registered "pure and simple, with no modifications, restrictions, or other clause which undermines or impedes their full execution. . . ."[17] Although sapped by the disasters of Louis' last years, such doctrine still governed relations between crown and Parlement in 1715. But regencies were traditionally times of royal weakness, and the magistrates hoped to regain their constitutional ground. Their confidence was not misplaced.

II

By 1715 the magistrates of the Parlement of Paris had evolved into the distinct and clearly defined category of *gens de la robe longue*. They were securely perched at the very top of a long and complex ladder of both bourgeois and nobility of the robe. Beginning with the bourgeois country notaries, and ascending through various ranks of solicitors, barristers, judges, and prosecutors, a long social trail wound upward to the thirty-one sovereign courts of France, with the Parlement of Paris at the pinnacle. To be sure, most of the tribe were obscure provincial bourgeois, whose path of advancement was blocked by modest means and the lack of influential connections. But near the top the social complexion of the legal profession became aristocratic. Magistrates of the sovereign courts, and some individuals below, had purchased nobility, which created an additional barrier separating the *gens de la robe longue* from their inferiors.

The laws of the realm, no less than social custom, supported the position of the magistrates of the Parlement of

[16] Isambert and others (eds.), *Recueil général*, XVIII, 103–80.
[17] *Ibid.*, XIX, 70–73.

Paris. The establishment of the *Paulette* in 1604 had given the judges a qualified ownership of office, with tenure made more secure by the crown's chronic lack of cash. This ownership of office grew throughout the reign of the Sun King into an unquestioned right, and other privileges were added to it. In 1690 Louis XIV added new offices to his Parlement and gave these places the confirmation of nobility, thus ennobling any commoner who happened to buy one. He could not long resist extending this privilege to the rest of the offices of the Parlement, which he did in 1704. Five years later he confirmed the magistrates in the right of hereditary succession, allowing them to sell or will their positions as they chose, without fee or hindrance from the crown.[18] Excepting the wholly theoretical right of the crown to repurchase the offices, by 1715 the magistrates had obtained outright ownership of their positions and were exempt from royal removal. A group of office-holders had been converted into an administrative caste.

[18] "Arrest du Conseil d'Etat du Roy et Déclaration du Roy contenant la dispense des quarante jours accordée par Sa Majesté en faveur de tous les officiers de ce royaume qui en voudront jouir en payant par chacun an quatre deniers pour livre de la valeur et estimation de leurs offices suivant les estats qui en seront arrestez au Conseil de Sadite Majesté," B.N., série F 21555 (53), December, 1604. "Edit du Roy portant création de deux présidens, 16 conseillers, et autres officiers au Parlement de Paris . . . avec attribution du titre noble et d'exemption des droits seigneuriaux," B.N., série F 23614 (887), November, 1690. "Déclaration du Roy portant confirmation de la noblesse, exemption des droits seigneuriaux et autres privilèges, donnée en faveur des conseillers du Roy et substituts de M. le Procureur-Général du Roy au Parlement de Paris, comme estans du corps de la Cour," B.N., série F 23617 (700), June 29, 1704. "Edit du Roy portant amortissement du . . . annuel du denier 16 en faveur des officiers qui y sont sujets, et que tous qui estoient casuels et héréditaires, gages, taxations, augmentations de gages et autres droits y joints seront à l'avenir possedés à titre de survivance et ordonne la levée de la fixation de tous les offices," B.N., série F 23619 (682), December, 1709.

Of the magistrates who sat in the Regency Parlement, all but a very few were nobles when they assumed office. The vast majority had family connections within the magistrature; most, indeed, were the direct descendants of judicial officials. As the right of hereditary succession was used and the number of offices within the Parlement did not increase in the eighteenth century, this trend of rather tight caste formation continued. Not all of the magisterial families of the Parlement, of course, confined themselves to judicial careers and alliances—far from it. The eighteenth century saw magistrates and their sons enter other careers, notably the royal administrative service.[19] But it is clear that by the Regency it had become difficult to rise into the Parlement of Paris from below without the benefit of a fortunate marriage or bequest. The high robe, supported by legal definition and inherited position and wealth, was an administrative fact. And the substantial magistrates of the Parlement of Paris were the showpiece of the robe.

The institutional identification shared by all the magistrates of the Parlement of Paris did not obliterate distinctions of wealth and social position. It is easy enough to think of the *parlementaires* as fitting very neatly into a single social caste. An immediate assumption is made: Since the magistrates belong to the same company, they are the same in all social attributes. Being so similar, they must differ from everyone else. Office in the Parlement is a veil that covers and renders insignificant all social distinctions. This assumption is false and dangerous.

[19] The careers and genealogies of all the magistrates of the Parlement of Paris under Louis XV are contained in the excellent book by J. F. Bluche, *L'Origine des magistrats du Parlement de Paris au XVIIIe siècle* (Paris, 1956).

Office in the Parlement did not automatically make one
a millionaire, or courtier, or salon wit, or anything else.
Men from many social ranks coexisted within the Parlement. The genial academician President Hénault, lover
of Madame du Deffand and friend of Louis XV's Queen,
lived his life at the royal court and barely recognized his
colleague, the obscure bourgeois substitute Jean-Baptiste
Catherinet. The social gap between the millionaire Jean-
Antoine de Mesmes, First President of the Parlement, and
the obscure councilor Louis Guillaume Chubéré was gigantic. One can hardly overestimate the social differences
between the powerful and wealthy *présidents à mortier*
and the minor junior councilors of the Chambers of Request. The weighty magistrates were rich and important,
while the obscure differed from their bourgeois neighbors
only in title. The social differences between members of
the Parlement were fully as significant as those between
a peer at Versailles and a country gentleman from Fréjus.
Owning an office in the Parlement meant simply a position
in the upper ranks of the legal profession. Its social con-
notations were strictly limited; the law was a profession,
not a nation. The term "robe" signified a job, not a rank
in society, and to think otherwise is a fantasy.

The old and easy distinctions between robe and sword
can be overworked, but they still had some validity during
the Regency. Although broken up by Louis' death, the
court of Versailles was of very recent memory, and the
honorific distinctions of court position still had meaning.
Those who held them still lived, drew their pensions, and
even managed to retain some of their social influence.
The circle of courtiers began to disperse, but it did not
disappear. The peers, marshals, and cardinals, the *no-*

blesse de race and their clients all did their best to stay in Paris near the Regent and his purse and uphold the honors and distinctions they had won at Versailles.[20]

Among these proud holders of honorific distinctions few magistrates were numbered. The magistrates had lived in Paris and the courtiers at Versailles, a day's journey in the seventeenth century. The magistrates worked hard at their profession; the Parlement opened at seven in the morning and closed at six in the evening. It was impossible for a judge in the Parlement to have any honorific position that demanded his presence with the King at Versailles. It was equally difficult for a magistrate to appear assiduously at Versailles in order to be noticed by Louis and qualify for these honors and pensions. Distance further prevented intimate social gatherings from breaking down the barriers of honor and employment. The nobles of Versailles derived their prestige from their names, their military commands, and their courtly titles and honors. They were bound to a feudal, military, or perhaps courtier tradition. There is no judgment to be made here; such a tradition was neither more nor less noble than the judicial and bureaucratic one of the magistrates of the high robe. But it was different.

All of these differences can be symbolically summed up in so simple a thing as the names and titles of the robe and the sword. The First President of the Parlement of Paris, Jean-Antoine de Mesmes, was called by his associates and enemies alike "M. le Premier Président de Mesmes." He was also the Count of Avaux and could quite properly have been addressed "M. le comte d'Avaux." Although correct in itself, this did not convey

[20] See the always provocative and frequently brilliant book by Franklin Ford, *Robe and Sword* (Cambridge, Mass., 1953).

the fact that de Mesmes was the First President of the Parlement of Paris, something far more important in the eyes of his contemporaries than any other title he might have.

Just the opposite could be seen at the royal court. Only a few, such as "M. le Premier" and "M. le Grand," the First and Grand Equerries of France, were addressed by the names of their offices. The rest bore the names of their estates. The Duke of Saint-Simon, a peer of France, was never called "M. de Rouvroy," his family name. That would have been scandalous. He was always "M. de Saint-Simon," by the title of his estate and peerage. What pertained for Saint-Simon was equally true for the rest of the secular nobility of the royal court, in fact, for the non-judicial nobility in general. Their identification was with their titles and estates; that of the robe was with their offices.

The differences between robe and sword, however, were neither impassible nor absolute. The social gulf between Paris and Versailles existed, and no one doubted it, but it was bridged with increasing frequency. Saint-Simon went into paroxyms of rage when his brother-in-law, the Duke of Lorges, married the daughter of First President de Mesmes, and he finally refused to attend the ceremony. But this was an archaic attitude. The lure of the magistrate's money was too much for the impoverished courtier to resist, and the de Mesmes family was older than that of Saint-Simon himself. It was a good marriage, and it took place with the Regent himself signing the marriage contract.[21]

[21] Saint-Simon, *Mémoires,* XXXVIII, 61–68; Mathieu Marais, *Journal et Mémoires sur la Régence et le règne de Louis XV,* ed. M. de Lescure (Paris, 1863–68), II, 11.

If the social gap between the Parlement of Paris and Versailles was narrowing, however, another was growing steadily wider, and by 1715 had been apparent to everyone for a long time. This was the growing difference between the magistrates of the Parlement and the rest of the legal profession. There had been a time, between 1520 and 1650, when the ancestors of the Regency magistrates first obtained their offices and were still bourgeois. By 1715, however, this was forgotten, or at least the magistrates were trying very hard to forget it. Occasional critics like Saint-Simon would remind them, but the high robe was clearly a distinct part of the Second Estate. The increasing pace of assimilation of the magistrature with the sword had serious consequences for the Parlement. Its judges were more and more men whose fathers had held office in a sovereign court or who had married into a magisterial family. The rise of the bourgeois into the Parlement diminished greatly, because there were fewer places for sale to new men. When President Bailleul sold his office in 1718, for 350,000 *livres*, it was to Germain Louis Chauvelin, a scion of a magisterial family. By the end of the century this would reach immense proportions, but it was clear enough during the Regency. The titled magistrate less and less resembled the lawyer pleading before him and came to look to Versailles as the object of his ambitions.

III

The Parlement of Paris was primarily a court of law. The oldest and largest of the thirty-one sovereign courts of France, the Parlement began its independent operations in the thirteenth century. Closest to the King, the Parle-

ment enjoyed the enormous prestige accruing to the court
nearest the royal power. The King pled his own cases
there, and the peerage of France sat in the Parlement.
The *ressort,* or judicial district, of the Parlement of Paris
covered over half of France. The Parlement was the highest appellate court of the realm, the last step in the complex and twisted ladder of appeals that began in thousands
of municipal and manorial tribunals, the apex of the still
medieval judicial system of Old Regime France.[22]

The Parlement was created and sustained for law, and
law rather than politics filled the magistrates' day. The
Parlement's political powers were secondary and his-
torically accidental, but its legal competence was not.
There was no doubt that the Parlement had begun as an
outgrowth of the King's council, organized to handle the
growing pressure of judicial business. The great bulk of
the huge number of cases before the Parlement were appeals from various lower courts—*présidial,* municipal, special royal tribunals, and even manorial courts. The 160
magistrates tried valiantly to keep up with this flood of
litigation. In addition to this, the Parlement was the
court of first instance for the King, the peerage, and those
who held the prized letters of *committimus,* entitling them
to a hearing in the court.[23] This mass of law is reflected in

---

[22] The *ressort* of the Parlement of Paris in 1715 included: Picardy,
Brie, Champagne, Ile-de-France, Perche, Beauce, Maine, Touraine,
Sologne, Berry, Nivernais, Anjou, Poitou, Aunis, Rochelois, Angoumois,
La Marche, Bourbonnais, Mâconnais, Auvergne, Forez, Beaujolais, and
Lyonnais.

[23] A letter of *committimus* entitled the holder to have his case tried
in the Parlement in the first instance. Given to the peerage and to
the magistrates of the Parlement, such a document was a highly valued
possession. The cost of justice was so great, and the delays so lengthy,
that a letter of *committimus* was the most valuable legal insurance
one could have.

the gigantic archives of the Parlement, the largest single corpus for the Old Regime, and in the intolerable delay in legal proceedings.

The law provided the magistrates' income. Although politics was spectacular and flattered the magistrates' self-esteem, it was not remunerative. There was no financial profit from political life. In fact, there was loss, for politics cut down on the time spent with the business of law, and the law paid well. The process of an appeal to the Parlement cost a great deal. The magistrates who heard the case received a fee. Each document drawn up in the Parlement cost the clients further. Added to this was the *épices* system, the practice of bribing magistrates to hasten justice. Finally, the length of the judicial process, often stretching over years and even generations, assured the magistrates a continuing income.

The Parlement was organized internally to administer justice.[24] It was divided into eight permanent chambers and two additional bodies with revolving membership. Each had separate identity, functions, and personnel. At the administrative head of the Parlement was the *Grand' Chambre*, the most venerable and powerful section of the court. The First President was its chief officer. He sat upon a throne, directed the deliberations of his collagues, and conferred with the King and the *gens du Roi*. Jean de Mesmes, the Regency First President, was a good example of the species. He came from a powerful parlementary family with long antecedents in the Parlement. Genial, clever, immensely rich, and accomplished as a courtier, he was a valuable link between court and crown. Appointed by the King and serving at his pleasure,

[24] See Marcel Marion, *Dictionnaire des institutions de la France aux XVIIe et XVIIIe siècles* (Paris, 1923), 422–33.

the First President could hardly afford to ignore the crown. A member of the Parlement dependent for his effectiveness on the good will of his colleagues, he could not dismiss their opinions to follow the King's. The position called for patience and diplomacy, and de Mesmes had both.

Scarcely less powerful were the eight *présidents à mortier*, who sat in the *Grand' Chambre* and took their name from the inverted chemist mortar shape of their hats. Rich and important, with long service in the Parlement, these men helped the First President direct the labors of the court. From their ranks came the First President, and, occasionally, ministers of the King. The councilors of the *Grand' Chambre*, both lay and cleric, were the judges who had been in the Parlement the longest. Supported and guided by their *présidents à mortier*, the *Grand' Chambre* councilors had an immense influence on both the First President and the rest of the court.

The *Grand' Chambre* claimed to be the original Parlement of Saint Louis, the rest of the court being merely administrative offshoots put out from time to time as the work load increased. Its predominance within the Parlement was unchallenged. The most important and lucrative cases came to the *Grand' Chambre*, and the political positions of the Parlement were decided here. It was in the *Grand' Chambre* that the peers of France sat, and here that the King pled. Through his *gens du Roi*, the King had his opinions and desires presented to the Parlement. The procurer-general and the two advocates-general were the crown's legal representatives in the Parlement, and major cases required their opinion. They spoke on the registration of edicts. They defended the King's rights, and their functions and importance were hardly less than those of the First President.[25]

While it was the center of the Parlement, the *Grand' Chambre* was not all of it. There were five Chambers of Inquests and two Chambers of Requests, each with a fixed number of magistrates, both presidents and councilors. Both Inquests and Requests had specific duties. The Chambers of Inquests examined appeals, read the written briefs of the lawyers in such cases, conducted investigations, and questioned local and provincial legal officials. Most of the heavy and often tiresome and routine legal work was carried on in the Chambers of Inquests. The two Chambers of Requests dealt with cases arising from the letters of *committimus*, in which the Parlement was a court of first instance. In both the Inquests and Requests sat the younger and less experienced magistrates. They were also the most radical politically, and often during the Regency de Mesmes was unable to contain revolts from these chambers.

There were also bodies with rotating membership. One of these was the *Tournelle*, composed largely of men from the Inquests and Requests, which dealt with appeals in criminal matters. The Interim Chamber also had no fixed personnel. Serving from September 7 to November 12, Saint Martin's Day, each year, the Interim Chamber held

[25] During the Regency the *gens du Roi* were:

> PROCURER-GENERAL: Henri François d'Aguesseau, 1715–February, 1717; Guillaume François Joly de Fleury, February, 1717–1723
>
> FIRST ADVOCATE-GENERAL: Guillaume François Joly de Fleury, 1715–February, 1717; Guillaume de Lamoignon de Blancmesnil, February, 1717–1723
>
> SECOND ADVOCATE-GENERAL: Germain Louis Chauvelin, 1715–December, 1718; Pierre Gilbert de Voisins, December, 1718–1723

the fort while the rest of the Parlement enjoyed a holiday. This body was chaired by a *président à mortier*, with magistrates selected in turn to serve with him. As a rule, it did very little work, with all major cases being postponed until the return of the full session.

Organized for law, the magistrates were mostly judges. But, because of their traditions and political powers of registration, modification, and remonstrance, they had become politicians. From the elevation of the bench, and wrapped in the mysterious majesty of the law, the judges of the Parlement pursued their politics. Building on the traditions of the past, and setting the pattern for the future, the Regency Parlement of Paris gave reality to the magistrates' role of judicial politics.

CHAPTER II

The Formation
of the Regency

I

DURING THE SUMMER of 1715 the King's gentle decline became more rapid. By August 12 Louis was too ill to go out into the air. The next day he walked for the last time, to a *petite musique* in the apartments of Madame de Maintenon. Thereafter he remained in his bed or was carried to his appointments. It was obvious to all who cared to see that the King was dying. Still he kept up the vast, elaborate ceremonial of his daily life and retained his grave, majestic courtesy. Although bedridden, Louis had himself carried to the throne room and stood unaided through an audience with the Persian ambassador. The next day he held a Council of Finances and through the week worked as usual with his ministers. August 25 was the festival of Saint Louis, which the King ordered to proceed as usual. Drums and hautboys played beneath the King's window as he woke, and his orchestra performed as he ate a small dinner. Through all these days the Sun King kept up his state.

But the end was inexorable. Gangrene overcame his leg and spread to his body. His appetite was gone. At the last his courtiers left. On August 28 he lost consciousness, to regain it only intermittently thereafter. His desperate physicians even admitted a Provencal peasant to administer a potion to cure the King. But this pathetic reminder of a medieval past availed nothing. Louis continued to sink. On August 31 he received the last rites of the Church. The next day he died.

While the King retained consciousness, the courtiers remained in a vigil before the doors of his apartments. For a week and a half the courtiers watched, only to desert in flocks when he sank into a coma. The King's anterooms emptied, while those of the Duke of Maine, the royal designate for Regent, were filled with new friends. Even the Duke of Orléans, detested by the old King and court, enjoyed the attentions of new admirers. Ministers and diplomats scurried about uneasily. On the twenty-ninth the dying King regained consciousness for the day, and the whole court deserted their prospective patrons and masters and rushed back to the royal apartments to see and be seen at the miraculous cure of the Sun King. After his brief rally, the King sank into a final coma. The Sun King's successor was a five-year-old child. There would be a Regency.

While the Regent himself would probably be the first prince of the blood, the Duke of Orléans, rumor held that the power of the new government would be vested in a Council controlled by the favorite son, the illegitimate Duke of Maine. Indications of this had come already; on August 2, 1714, the Duke of Maine had been placed in the line of succession to the throne right after the Duke of Orléans.[1] It was whispered, also, that the Duke of Maine was prominently mentioned in the will of the Sun King. Courtiers and ministers began to choose sides for

---

[1] Text of the edict is in Isambert and others (eds.), *Recueil général,* XX, 619–23. The minutes of the registration are in Buvat, *Journal de la Régence,* I, 503–10.

the anticipated contest between the Duke of Maine and the Duke of Orléans for power in the rapidly approaching regency.

The actual provisions of the King's will were known by the Duke of Orléans before the death of the King. Accordingly he took measures to assure his succession to the power, as well as the title, of Regent. On August 30, two days before the death of the King, the Duke of Orléans sent a memoir to the First President of the Parlement, Jean de Mesmes, outlining his demands and the ways in which he would conciliate the Parlement.[2] He demanded the Regency on birth alone, as the first prince of the blood. The Duke of Orléans wished to name the members of the Council of Regency. He could not submit to majority rule in his own council. Further, the King's household troops must be commanded by the Regent. The governors and tutors of the new king were well chosen, but they should exercise their duties under the authority of the Regent. Finally, the Duke of Maine must be prohibited from taking the young King from place to place without the permission of the Regent and the Parlement. In return for this point by point emasculation of the King's will, the Duke of Orléans promised to "revoke by an edict the articles of the ordinances of 1667 and 1673 that kept the Court from making remonstrances; and, to make that edict immediately, he promised the continuation of the sittings of the Parlement for the register-

---

[2] "Mémoire donnée par M. le duc d'Orléans à quelqu'uns du parlement dès le jour de la mort du Roy," in Marais, *Journal et Mémoires,* I, 174–76. In his memoirs Saint-Simon said that the death of the King caught the Duke of Orléans by surprise. It is hard to see how this could have been the case, as the King had been dying for weeks. In any event, this statement of Saint-Simon is disproved by the existence of Marais' memoir. For Saint-Simon's opinions see Saint-Simon, *Mémoirs,* XXIX, 103.

ing of that edict and for public affairs until the end of September." [3] When de Mesmes received this, he called the *présidents à mortier* to a meeting at the Palais de Justice. He read "a memoir, in which the duc d'Orléans made proposals, and without committing himself to anything, he remarked simply . . . that the duc d'Orléans ought to be subjected to the majority vote in the Council of Regency. He added that he would reply only that it would be the subject of deliberations, and we would consider it. The others said nothing. . . ." [4] The little meeting was quite revealing. The First President belonged to the party of the Duke of Maine; the silence of the other presidents indicated that they were partisans of the Duke of Orléans. Certainly Aligre was; he thought the Duke of Orléans' rights to the Regency were incontestable. [5]

The Duke of Orléans was not the only one taking precautions. The peers of France were also making plans to protect their rights. The first of these was known as the "bonnet," the right of a peer to remain covered when addressing a president of the Parlement and of having the president uncover when addressing a peer. The second was the complaint of the peers that councilors of the Parlement were sitting on the peers' benches. [6]

[3] "Mémoire donnée par M. le duc d'Orléans," in Marais, *Journal et Mémoires,* I, 176.

[4] Etienne d'Aligre, "Relation de ce qui se passa au Parlement de Paris à la mort de Louis XIV," *Revue Rétrospective,* 2nd series, VI (1836), 7. For the career of Aligre see Bluche, *L'Origine des magistrats,* 58–59.

[5] M. Anthoine, *Journal de la maladie et de la mort de Louis XIV,* ed. E. Drummont (Paris, 1880), 137; Aligre, "Relation," 13; A. Langlois, "Ancêtres des parlementaires parisiens," *Bulletin de la Société de l'histoire de Paris et de l'Ile-de-France,* LIII (1926), 62.

[6] Saint-Simon, *Mémoires,* XXIX, 3–6; Louis de Rouvroy, Duke of

Accordingly, as soon as he heard of the death of the King, the Duke of Saint-Simon, leader of the peers' struggle for their rights, went with eleven or twelve others to visit the Duke of Orléans. They reminded him of his promise to decide in favor of the peers on the question of the "bonnet." [7] The Duke of Orléans, embarrassed by the visit, begged the peers not to disturb so important a meeting. He "agreed many times that the bonnet was a frightful usurpation and that the other grievances that plagued us were not less, but he wished to pick the time and place, and not trouble so important a meeting by an individual quarrel." Saint-Simon argued that the Duke of Orléans would sacrifice the private interests of the peers for good, that once the sitting had gone in his favor he would forget the claims of the peers. The Duke of Orléans protested against this, and "engaged us his positive word, formally and solemnly, to judge in our favor all disputes on the usurpation of the Parlement; hat, councilor on the bench, etc., as soon as the public affairs were settled." [8] This was the best Saint-Simon could do.

The Duke of Orléans' precautions did not end with the discouragement of the peers and a political bribe to the Parlement to insure himself of its support. At dawn of the day of the sitting the Palais de Justice was surrounded by 3,000 men of the French Guards, commanded by the

---

Saint-Simon, "Explication du plan de la Grand' Chambre du Parlement de Paris," *Ecrits inédits de Saint-Simon*, ed. A. P. Faugère (Paris, 1881–93), IV, 461–73.

[7] Saint-Simon, *Mémoires*, XXIX, 3.

[8] *Ibid.*, 6; Comte de Clairambault, "Relation de la séance au Parlement du 2 septembre 1715," Manuscrits français, B.N., No. 719. According to Boislisle, who is extremely reliable, this was possibly written by Saint-Simon. See Saint-Simon, *Mémoires*, XXIX, Appendix 1, 467.

Duke of Guiche, who received 600,000 *livres* from the Duke of Orléans for this service. Elite soldiers and many officers were in the interior of the Palais itself, and soldiers occupied the street from the Pont Neuf to the Pont St. Michel.[9] The magistrates, entering the Palais before six in the morning, were very displeased when they met the troops. The Duke of Orléans appeased them by saying that the troops were not a precaution against the Parlement, although to a certain extent they probably were, but against the Duke of Maine, who commanded the Swiss.[10] Clearly all was ready as far as the Duke of Orléans could manage it for the vital sitting of September 2, 1715.

II

At six-thirty on the morning of September 2 the meeting of the Parlement of Paris began.[11] The First President spoke of the pretensions of the peers who wished to ignore former usage and remain covered when answering a president of the Parlement. Did "the gentlemen of the Parlement judge it proper to take no notice of this now, in order not to impede the affairs which ought to be discussed, and later take new measures against the peers, or resist it openly?"[12] The gentlemen wished to resist. If the peer spoke with his hat on, the First President was to tell him that his vote did not count and then pass on

[9] Marais, *Journal et Mémoires*, I, 183; Saint-Simon, *Mémoires*, XXIX, 18; Don H. Leclercq, *Histoire de la Régence* (Paris, 1922), I, 101–102; P. E. Lemontey, *Histoire de la Régence et de la minorité de Louis XV* (Paris, 1832), I, 35.

[10] Aligre, "Relation," 22.

[11] The official registers of the session are printed in Buvat, *Journal de la Régence*, I, 479–502; Isambert and others (eds.), *Recueil général*, XXI, 1–25; Flammermont (ed.), *Les Remontrances*, I, 3–30.

[12] Aligre, "Relation," 8.

to the next peer. Thus the peers would be forced to conform to the magistrates' views or be unable to vote.[13]

At nine-thirty the Duke of Orléans arrived. As he crossed the floor he spoke to the peers, asking them not to raise the question of their privileges and interrupt important affairs of state. No sooner was he seated, however, than the peers did just that. Saint-Simon cried that the Duke of Orléans ought to render justice to the peerage immediately. The Archbishop of Rheims rose and read a formal protest from the peerage. Embarrassed, the Duke of Orléans turned at once to the First President, assuring him that he had begged the peers not to raise the question of their rights and disrupt the session. He asked that the incident be forgotten. De Mesmes retorted that it would not affect the rights of the peers, if they had any.[14] Then the business of the session began.

The First President welcomed the Duke of Orléans to the Parlement and did not even mention his rival the Duke of Maine. Pleased with this, and sensing victory already, the Duke of Orléans decided to make his major proposals. Speaking confidently, he told the court of the

[13] *Ibid.*, 11; "Relation de la séance au Parlement du 2 septembre 1715," Manuscrits français, B.N., No. 719; M. de Corbéron, "Récit de ce qui s'est passé au Parlement de Paris après la mort de Louis le Grand pour l'établissement de la régence pendant la minorité du Roy Louis XV," in Saint-Simon, *Mémoires*, XXIX, Appendix 1, 484; Marais, *Journal et Mémoires*, I, 158.

[14] Anthoine, *Journal de la maladie*, 143; "Relation," 11; "Lettre contenant la relation de ce qui s'est passé à la mort de Louis XIV et à l'occasion du lit de justice pour la Régence," quoted in Marquis de Dangeau, *Journal*, ed. Soulie and Dussieux (Paris, 1854–60), XVIII, Appendix 4, 370–80. See Marais, *Journal et Mémoires*, I, 160, for the text of the speech. According to Saint-Simon, he himself, and not the Archbishop of Rheims, made this speech. No other observer agrees with him; all say it was the archbishop. For Saint-Simon's story see Saint-Simon, *Mémoires*, XXIX, 14–18.

last words Louis XIV had spoken to him. The late King had said, ". . . my nephew, I have made a will in which I have given you all the rights of your birth. I commend the Dauphin to you; serve him as faithfully as you have served me, work to conserve his Kingdom for him; if he comes to grief, you will be the master and the Crown will belong to you. I have made the dispositions I believe best, but as one cannot foresee all, if anything is wrong it ought to be changed." [15] Then the duke went on to amplify his opening wedge:

Those are his own words. I am thus convinced that following the laws of the Kingdom . . . and the will of the late King, the Regency belongs to me. But I will not be satisfied . . . if you do not join your suffrage and approbation, with which I will not be less flattered than with the Regency itself. Thus I ask you, when you have read the testament of the late King, and the codicils I have brought you, do not confuse my different

[15] Flammermont (eds.), *Les Remontrances*, I, 6; Buvat, *Journal de la Régence*, I, 482; Marais, *Journal et Mémoires*, I, 160–61; Corbéron, "Récit," 484; Fevret de Fontette, "Relation de ce qui s'est passé au Parlement de Paris au sujet de la régence et gouvernement du Roy Louis XV," in Saint-Simon, *Mémoires*, XXIX, Appendix I, 490–91; Chevalier de Poissens, *Mémoires de la Régence* (The Hague, 1729), I, 3; Lemontey, *Histoire de la Régence et de la minorité de Louis XV*, I, 35. Lemontey says these words of Louis XIV were a fabrication, "without truth or witness." I am inclined to agree with this opinion, for the dying King was seldom alone; and, other than in Poissens' *Mémoires*, they are not mentioned except in the speech of the Duke of Orléans. Marais and Corbéron give the substance of the speech; the registers and Fevret quote; but all heard the duke give his speech. Poissens has, I feel, picked up the current gossip and included it in his memoirs. He does not quote; he merely says that the Duke of Orléans was able to get only vague promises from Louis XIV. There is no doubt then that the duke reported that Louis XIV said these words, but there is quite a bit of doubt that Louis actually did say them. Fabrication or not, however, they echoed the prevailing sentiment of the court and served their purpose.

claims . . . on the right my birth gives me, and that which the testament will add to it. I am persuaded you will judge it proper to begin on the first. But to the various claims that I have by right to the Regency, I dare to assure you Gentlemen, that I will merit it by my zeal for the service of the King, by my love for the public good, above all aided by your council and your wise remonstrances. I protest before this august assembly that I will never have any other design than to ease the people, re-establish good order in the finances, retrench superfluous expenses, establish peace inside and outside the Kingdom, above all to re-establish the union and tranquility of the Church, and to work with all possible application to render the state happy and flourishing.[16]

A murmur of approval swept the court following this speech of the first prince of the blood. Being consulted on important affairs of state and having the right of remonstrance returned were happy and welcome changes from the stern distrust of the Sun King. It is little wonder that President Aligre wrote that the Duke of Orléans spoke "with presence of spirit, with wisdom, with politeness, with consideration for the dignity of the Parlement. . . ."[17] It is less wonder that the magistrates agreed with the *gens du Roi,* who felt that the Duke of Orléans ought, by his birth and abilities, to be elevated to the full powers of Regent. The struggle of the Regency was all but over, and the Duke of Maine had not even opened his mouth.

It was not possible, however, to completely ignore the will of Louis XIV. Everyone thought that the will and the codicils should be read, and even the Duke of Orléans, who had reason to fear them, made no objection. The

[16] Buvat, *Journal de la Régence,* I, 482–83; Isambert and others (eds.), *Recueil général,* XXI, 4–5; Flammermont (ed.), *Les Remontrances,* I, 6–7; Anthoine, *Journal de la maladie,* 81, 143; Aligre, "Relation," 11; Corbéron, "Récit," 484; Marais, *Journal et Mémoires,* I, 160–61.
[17] Aligre, "Relation," 11.

main provisions of the will concerned the establishment and composition of the Regency and the care and education of the young King. Here the favor of Louis XIV for his illegitimate son was as clear as his distrust of the Duke of Orléans. There was to be a Council of Regency composed of the princes of the blood and chief officers of the crown. The education and guardianship of Louis XV were to be under the authority of this council, and the Duke of Maine was specifically charged to see that this was done properly. Most important was the question of authority in the Council of Regency. All of the council's decisions were to be approved by a strict majority vote, and no action could be taken by the Regent alone. Finally, the rights of succession of the Duke of Maine were maintained, and the composition of the Council of Regency could be changed only with the assent of the majority of the members.[18] The Sun King had envisioned a Regency without a Regent.

After the reading of the will there was unhappy surprise among the listeners, except for the Duke of Orléans and the Duke of Maine, who knew what to expect. The magistrates had been misled by the Duke of Orléans about the contents of the will and the wishes of the late King. Their indignation was turned toward the late King, however, for few of them were friends of the Duke of Maine. Moreover, they wished to regain the right of remonstrance. The Duke of Orléans spoke immediately in an attempt to efface the impressions made by the will. In spite of the respect he had for the wishes of the late King, he felt that the will infringed upon the rights of

[18] Text of the will is in Leclercq, *Histoire de la Régence*, I, 108–12; Claude Louis Hector Villars, *Mémoires*, ed. Marquis de Vogüe (Paris, 1884–1904), IV, 66–72.

his birth. The last words which the late King had spoken to him contradicted the will, and he insisted that the Parlement render an opinion on his right of birth before discussing the articles of the will.[19] His preparation for the session was to be put to the test. The advice of the *gens du Roi* on the Duke of Orléans' demand was entirely favorable. They reported that if the will of the late King gave only the title and not the power of Regent, "it was necessary to think more of the spirit than the letter of the will. . . ."[20] The magistrates concurred and named the Duke of Orléans Regent by acclamation rather than by formal vote.[21] The struggle for power in a Regency, which in 1610 and 1648 had proved so serious and prolonged, ended in one hour in 1715. The potential intrigue and factional strife was reduced to a minimum, and the transition from the Sun King to a Regency was smooth and swift. Victory for the Duke of Orléans, not unexpected in view of his birth and preparations, was achieved with the first blow.

With the tide running so rapidly in his favor, the new Regent rose to speak again. Now he felt strong enough to press for even more. He outlined his plan to create councils to replace the old secretaries of state, who had been the ministers under Louis XIV. He modestly claimed that he needed the wisdom and experience of others. Therefore, in accordance with the plans of the

---

[19] Buvat, *Journal de la Régence*, I, 486; Anthoine, *Journal de la maladie*, 146; Aligre, "Relation," 14–15; Marais, *Journal et Mémoires*, I, 163–64; Corbéron, "Récit," 486; M. Prévot, "Relation de ce que s'est passé au Parlement (après la mort de Louis XIV) par M. Prévot, avocat," in Saint-Simon, *Mémoires*, XXIX, Appendix I, 478.

[20] Flammermont (ed.), *Les Remontrances*, I, 11–13; Buvat, *Journal de la Régence*, I, 486–88; Prévot, "Relation par M. Prévot," 479.

[21] Anthoine, *Journal de la Maladie*, 137. Prévot, "Relation par M. Prévot," 479, says much the same thing.

late and very popular dauphin, the Duke of Burgundy, he was going to abolish the secretaries of state and replace them with councils, all to be supervised by the Council of Regency. Here men from the other councils would sit and give expert advice. The Regent added that he lacked experience and would voluntarily submit himself to the rulings of his Council of Regency, but he wished to be able to appoint to that council whom he wished. In addition to this, he wanted command of all the household troops of the King.[22]

It was only now that the Duke of Maine was allowed to speak. During the course of the morning he had seen his position reduced to almost nothing. Unprepared for the session, he now paid the price. He had neglected to bribe the Parlement, had failed to assure the loyalty of the troops, and had not gotten the support of the peers and princes of the blood. Having relied entirely on the respect which might be shown for the will of Louis XIV, he had failed to understand the antagonism of the magistrates to the Sun King; nor had he sensed the decline in awe and respect toward the late monarch in his last, disastrous years. He had not known how many were waiting for Louis XIV to die. He had been too close, too attached in interest and affection to the dead King, and he had miscalculated. It was fatal for his chances in the Regency.

Rising to speak, the Duke of Maine said that he had known there would be trouble when the late King had destined him for the high post of Commandant of the Troops of the King's household. He had even told Louis XIV as much, but the King had admonished him to re-

[22] Buvat, *Journal de la Régence*, I, 488–90; Flammermont (ed.), *Les Remontrances*, I, 13–15; Prévot, "Relation par M. Prévot," 479; Anthoine, *Journal de la Maladie*, 146–47; Aligre, "Relation," 14–16, Marais, *Journal et Mémoires*, I, 164–66.

spect his wishes. He would now be glad to sacrifice his interests to those of the state; he only wanted the Parlement to firmly guarantee him the prerogatives to which he was entitled. He added that he had only the vain appearance of guarding the young King but had not the troops to do it adequately.[23] This was hardly the speech of a man aggressively seeking his rights, but rather an attempt to concede gracefully. The concession was accepted, again by acclamation. The political powers of the Duke of Maine were finished before they had even begun, to the great relief of that rather indolent prince, who had never wanted to play a political role in the first place.[24] Its main business completed after sitting continuously for over six hours, the Parlement recessed for lunch, to reconvene in the late afternoon.[25]

[23] Flammermont (ed.), *Les Remontrances,* I, 15–16; Buvat, *Journal de la Régence,* I, 490–91; Aligre, "Relation," 17–18; Corbéron, "Récit," 487; Anthoine, *Journal de la Maladie,* 147–48.

[24] Flammermont (ed.), *Les Remontrances,* I, 16–19; Buvat, *Journal de la Régence,* I, 493–94; Anthoine, *Journal de la Maladie,* 148.

[25] Aligre, "Relation," 16; Prévot, "Relation par M. Prévot, 480. Saint-Simon gives a long and detailed description of what happened after the decision was made to adjourn and before the sitting actually came to an end. He says that the Regent rose to attack the codicils. The Duke of Maine interrupted him, and the two had a public quarrel in front of the Parlement. Seeing that this undignified spectacle would injure the cause of his friend the new Regent, Saint-Simon motioned him into the fourth Chamber of Inquests, off the *Grand' Chambre.* The Regent would not go, and continued arguing. Saint-Simon finally persuaded the Regent to stop and to suspend the sitting as had already been agreed. The Regent then apologized to the Parlement for having kept it so long and promised to give it the right to remonstrate. At this point the session ended.

See Saint-Simon, *Mémoires,* XXIX, 21–29. Substantially the same story is found in Louis de Rouvroy, Duke of Saint-Simon, "Additions au Journal de Marquis de Dangeau," in Dangeau, *Journal,* XVI, 65–72. Other accounts indicate where Saint-Simon got the basis of his story. Marais, *Journal et Mémoires,* I, 166, says that the Regent went into

When the session opened about four o'clock, the new Regent again took the floor, resolved to press home the plan of governmental reorganization he had introduced earlier. In addition to the Council of Regency, the Regent felt there should be several other councils—for war, finance, marine affairs, foreign affairs, and religion—composed of men attached to the good of the kingdom. Thus the ministerial tyranny of the previous reign would be ended, and the greatest and most influential men of France would again be consulted on the affairs of state. He concluded with a final plea for his own power. All offices and benefices, that is all patronage, must belong to the Regent alone. And all the troops of France, even those of the King's household, must be commanded by the Regent. In short, the Regent "wished to be free to do good, and he consented to be bound in order not to do evil." With that happy phrase, applauded by all, he concluded and asked for the opinions of the magistrates.

---

the fourth Chamber of Inquests and talked with the *gens du Roi.* Clairambault, "Relation de la séance au Parlement du 2 septembre 1715," Manuscrits français, B.N., No. 719, mentions this, and adds that the Regent talked with the Duke of Maine. No spectacular quarrel was mentioned. The other sources—the official registers, Aligre, Anthoine, Prévot, Corbéron, Fevret, Buvat—do not mention this quarrel, so public and so spectacular.

It seems strange, if Saint-Simon's story were true, that the Parlement would forget it had been given the right to remonstrate and that every other chronicler of the *lit de justice* would overlook so important a public fight between two of the realm's highest nobles. But such appears to be the case. Although Leclercq, a major authority on the Regency, accepted Saint-Simon's version, I feel that the evidence is too flimsy. See Leclercq, *Histoire de la Régence,* I, 118–21. Saint-Simon wrote his memoirs in the 1740's, twenty-five years after the event, and is notoriously inaccurate. His unsupported word is not enough. Therefore, I have omitted this quarrel from the text entirely and have relied on the minutes of the sitting and the testimony of the other chroniclers of the event.

The magistrates could only have one opinion. Having given the Duke of Orléans so much, could they refuse him now? And would it mean anything if they did? Would not the new Regent merely take the powers he now so politely asked of the Parlement? Certainly, beyond any doubt. What then could the magistrates say of the last effort of the Duke of Maine, who rose now to speak? They brushed aside his final plea and voted to confirm to the Duke of Orléans all that he wished.[26] The Regent triumphed completely.

He then rose, thanked the First President and the magistrates for the honor they did him, and prepared to leave. To all appearances the session was ended. But the Regent could not resist one last word. He informed the magistrates that the peers had repeated to him their protest of the morning and that they wished a decision on whether a president should speak to a peer uncovered. The First President, considerably taken aback, merely repeated his earlier statement, that the peers would get their rights, if they had any.[27]

[26] Flammermont (ed.), *Les Remontrances*, I, 28; Marais, *Journal et Mémoires*, I, 169–70, 181–82; Fevret, "Relation au sujet de la régence," 493; Corbéron, "Récit," 488; Anthoine, *Journal de la Maladie*, 151; Aligre, "Relation," 19.

[27] Marais, *Journal et Mémoires*, I, 173. The following exchange between the Duke of Saint-Simon and President Potier de Novion, and later between the First President and Marshal Villars, is not in the official registers of the Parlement. Potier de Novion said the court would not put any complaints of the peers relating to the *affaire de bonnet* in its registers, and it did not. Nor did Saint-Simon mention this incident, so humiliating for him. However, if the principals did not record the exchange, all the numerous other witnesses did. See Aligre, "Relation," 20; Anthoine, *Journal de la Maladie*, 152; Marais, *Journal et Mémoires*, I, 171–72; Prévot, "Relation par M. Prévot," 482–83; Corbéron, "Récit," 489–90; Fevret, "Relation au sujet de la régence," 494–95. Clairambault, "Relation de la séance au Parlement du 2

This was too much for the Duke of Saint-Simon. Enraged at the failure of the peerage to win satisfaction, he leaped from his seat and cried, "Enscribe on your registers that the consideration of the Regent does nothing for us, for we are resolved, very resolved. . . ." [28]

President Potier de Novion interrupted: "No, Sir. We will not put a word on our registers."

"Act, act on our protests," cried Saint-Simon.

"To whom do you ask it; is it the Court?"

"Yes, the Court."

"Do you recognize the Court then as your judges?", asked Potier de Novion, closing the trap.

Horrified at his blunder, Saint-Simon could only stammer "No, no . . ." and sit down.

Marshal Villars tried to rescue the peers from Saint-Simon's mistake and embarrassment by relating a conversation he had had with the late King about the pretensions of the peers. The Marshal had told Louis XIV that it seemed odd that the presidents of the Parlement would not make the proper salute to the peers by uncovering when they spoke to them. The King had agreed and said that the situation ought to be corrected.[29] Immediately the First President jumped up and said that the late

septembre 1715," Manuscrits français, B.N., No. 719, gives long and precise details which support the other accounts. Collection Delisle, Archives Nationales, série U 359, September 2, 1715. Archives Nationales are hereinafter cited as A.N. "Relation de ce qui s'est passé au Parlement dans les deux séances du lundi 2 septembre 1715," in Saint-Simon, *Mémoires*, XXIX, Appendix 1, 496; "Note d'un manuscrit Caumartin," in Saint-Simon, *Mémoires*, XXIX, Appendix 1, 496–97.

[28] Marais, *Journal et Mémoires*, I, 172. The other sources do not mention this speech. However, it is the crux of the argument which all agree occurred, and, since Marais is generally very accurate, I have included it.

[29] Villars, *Mémoires*, IV, 62–63.

King had told him exactly the opposite. The Dean of the *Grand' Chambre,* Le Nain, added that the peers had taken off their hats for the last two hundred years and that there was no reason to change old usages. The session had become a mob scene, with magistrates, peers, and spectators milling around, arguing, and shoving. It was adjourned only by the abrupt departure of the Regent, who rapidly strode out by a side door. He was followed slowly by the crowd, still discussing the events of the day and speculating on those to come.

III

For the Parlement the political results of the triumph of September 2 were not long in coming. On September 15 the Regent kept his word concerning the right to remonstrate. He sent to the Parlement for registration an edict granting it the right to remonstrance. This "Declaration of Vincennes" stated:

. . . the fidelity, zeal and submission with which our court of Parlement has always served the King, our very honored lord and great-grandfather, engages us to give to it public marks of our confidence and above all in a time when the advice of a company as wise, as enlightened is able to be of so great use to us, we believe that we can do nothing more honorable for it and more advantageous for our own service than to permit it to represent to us what it judges necessary before proceeding to the registration of edicts and declarations that we address to it. We are persuaded that it will use with wisdom and circumspection the ancient liberty that we are re-establishing, that its advice will always tend to the good of the state and merits always to be confirmed by our authority. Because of this we wish that when we address to our Court of Parlement the ordinances, edicts, declarations and letters patent emanating from our authority, with our lettres de cachet ordering registration, our said Court, before proceeding to it, be able to represent to us that which it will judge apropos for the public good of our Kingdom. . . .[30]

The new Regent was a man who paid his debts.

The new addition of political power for the Parlement was only marginally significant in a strict institutional sense. The leverage added to the court's constitutional and political position was minute compared to that inherent in the right of registration. A remonstrance was, after all, only an optional auxiliary step in the procedure of refusing to register an edict. It might add or subtract from the Parlement's credit with the crown, but the right of registration, or the fact of being sent edicts to register, was the critical element in the court's politics. Viewed in these strictly legalistic and institutional terms, the Regent's gift was insubstantial indeed.

But it was not so viewed at the time. Both the magistrates and the Regent thought that he was offering real value for services received. No one entertained any doubt that the right of remonstrance was a vital element in the political powers of the Parlement. What the Parlement gained was not so much a new power, or the resurrection of an old power, but royal permission, and indeed encouragement, to use all its powers—registration, modification, and remonstrance alike. The Parlement's political

[30] Text is in Eusèbe J. de Laurière, *Recueil d'Edits et d'Ordonnances Royaux sur le fait de la justice et autres matières les plus importantes* (Paris, 1720), II, 499; Isambert and others (eds.), *Recueil général*, XXI, 40–41. Abridged text is in Leon Cahen, *Les Querelles religieuses et parlementaire sous Louis XV* (Paris, 1913), 18–19. See also text in "Registre des lettres patentes et ordonnances du Roy," A.N., série X (1A) 6714, fols. 746–47.

capabilities, dormant and suppressed under the Sun King, were to be revived. The Parlement was invited to actively re-enter political life.

Not only the Parlement, but the entire governmental organization of France seemed about to undergo a considerable change. The Regent clearly detested the Sun King's system of government, a view which accounted for what instant popularity he had. Everyone expected sweeping changes. Most privileged, articulate groups and persons hoped that the changes would be made in the direction of what might be called "legitimacy." Certainly the Regent himself appeared to think this way. Although Louis XIV had substituted a partially bureaucratic nexus for the personal ties of family, feudalism, and charter which had once bound subjects to the crown, the process was neither perfect nor finished at his death. Nor had the bureaucratic state received the complete approval of the magnates of the realm. Even in the palmy days of Colbert, the crown had had to struggle to make good the work and word of the bureaucracy against local charter, privilege, and custom. It had lost frequently.[31] More frequently the crown won a qualified victory, with the provincial or local institution conceding with ill grace. For all his power the Sun King was never able to extend royal control over the estates of Brittany, nor was the customs union of the *Cinq Gros Fermes* expanded to southern France. The tax system was never rationalized, nor was justice made uniform in spite of the efforts of Louis XIV.

[31] In this connection see the interesting monograph of Eugene Asher, *Resistance to the Maritime Classes: The Survival of Feudalism in the France of Colbert* (Berkeley, 1960), Vol. LXVI of the *University of California Publications in History*; Leon Bernard, "French Society and Popular Uprisings under Louis XIV," *French Historical Studies*, III, 454–75.

The bureaucratic state was still in the process of formation in 1715.

People complained about the new system, of course. Not merely those who opposed centralization and espoused local privilege, but some who favored the King were distressed at the failure of the King's bureaucracy to achieve justice and economy. With the War of the Spanish Succession these complaints became commonplace. Religious persecution, economic depression, war, and royal expenditure were laid at the door of the King and his agents. There was considerable unhappiness with the inefficiency and injustice of the bureaucracy. But more important, some took issue with the very process of centralization, which seemed to impinge on ancient local, corporate, and familial privileges. These immunities, while theoretically subject to the will of the King, they surrendered grudgingly, with loud protests and with every intention of regaining them. Now, with the death of the Sun King and the accession of a Regent who had disliked Louis' methods of government, the time had come for changes. The old, customary, and "legitimate" ways would be restored, and the new bureaucracy dismantled.

The line of claimants was long, and the Regent was to find that "legitimacy" for one was usurpation for others. He would also learn that the increased powers brought to the monarchy by the Sun King were valuable and ought to be retained. He would see that such schemes as reviving the claims of the Gallican Church or abolishing the ministries and substituting councils staffed by the peerage were hopelessly anachronistic and would fail utterly. But this was all in the future; September, 1715, was a time of vast optimism and confidence. And the Parlement, first in line, received its "legitimate," that is former, privileges, along with the permission to use them.

Many of the bargains and agreements made in 1715 were of short duration and vanished as the hard realities of governing France bore in on the Duke of Orléans. As a form of government, the councils of the *polysynodie* would be a total failure, and even the English alliance, so rightly prized by the Regent, was to evaporate in widespread colonial conflicts. But the Parlement's gains proved more durable and lasted throughout the rest of the Old Regime. The conflicts of the Regency, and they were numerous and bitter, did not end in a reduction of the court to silence and impotence. There was general agreement that the Parlement's claim to the rights of remonstrance and of a limited political voice was actually legitimate and ought to be respected. The conflicts of the Regency, and the rest of the Old Regime as well, with the one exception of the Maupeou Parlement, were less about whether the court ought to have a political voice than about what that voice ought to say. The political step of September 2, 1715, was permanent.

CHAPTER III

The Gallican Liberties
1715–18

SCARCELY HAD THE heart of the Sun King been taken by Cardinal Rohan to the Jesuits in Paris, when the religious quarrels of the previous reign broke out again. Cardinal Noailles, the Jansenist and Gallican Archbishop of Paris exiled from court in 1714, made a triumphal entry into favor on the very day of the death of the old King. Father le Tellier, Jesuit confessor to Louis XIV, was received with the coldest formality by the new Regent, who sent him away from the court to the jurisdiction of his society. Madame de Maintenon instantly retired to Saint Cyr. Persons near the throne responsible for the rigid orthodoxy of Louis XIV's declining years were in retreat and confusion.

Not merely cardinals and bishops, but even the people of the streets involved themselves. The Huguenots renewed their practice of attending services at the chapels of the Protestant ambassadors. As the body of Louis XIV was taken from Versailles to Paris, it was accompanied by the curses and taunts of those who saw it pass. A score of popular songs excoriated the Sun King, the Jesuits, and the religious politics of the previous era.[1] Paris showed itself to be Gallican and Jansenist.

[1] Emile Raunié (ed.), *Chansonnier historique du XVIIIe siècle* (Paris, 1879–84), I, 1–151.

One of the obvious focal points of the religious bickering was the Society of Jesus. As confessors to the late King, Father la Chaise and then Father le Tellier had been instrumental in obtaining royal support for the papal attack on the Gallicans and Jansenists. The Jesuits were popularly regarded as the trusted and cunning papal lieutenants in the struggle over orthodoxy. Following the revocation of the Edict of Nantes, orthodoxy had been one of the more important concerns of the crown. For the two years prior to Louis' death, orthodoxy, as measured by King and Jesuits, meant strict acceptance of the papal bull *Unigenitus*.

Clement XI had designed this bull, dated September 8, 1713, as a crushing blow against the Jansenists and all their works.[2] So strong and inclusive were its 101 articles that many who did not care at all about the theological merits of the argument felt that the bull pointed the way toward papal absolutism and the end of the Gallican liberties. By far the larger number of French opponents to the bull fell into this group. The bull fused French Jansenists and Gallicans into a single party. Most of the magistrates of the Parlement of Paris held strong Gallican views and opposed the papal bull.

There was not very much the Parlement could do about the bull while Louis XIV lived. On February 14, 1714, he sent *Unigenitus* to the Parlement with strict orders that it be registered. Extremely unhappy, but unable to resist the royal will, the magistrates had registered the bull, but only with the reservation that it be ". . . without prejudice to the liberties of the Gallican Church, rights

---

[2] Text of the bull is in Canon Dorsanne, *Journal contenant tout ce qui s'est passé à Rome et en France dans l'affaire de la Constitution "Unigenitus"* (Paris, 1753), I, 328–33.

and pre-eminence of the Crown, power and jurisdiction of the bishops of the Kingdom. . . ." [3]

The Sun King's acceptance of this mild reservation to the papal bull did not indicate any royal demur about the validity or propriety of the document. As long as he lived, Louis worked to eliminate any clerical opposition to *Unigenitus*. Having committed himself to the ultramontane position, he did his best to have it accepted everywhere, and he seemed to be succeeding. In anticipation of regal displeasure his critics were silent. But even Louis XIV could not live for ever; he died only eighteen months after the Parlement had registered the bull. The voices of dissent had been repressed, but the dissenters had not been converted.

With Louis XIV in his tomb the Gallicans took heart. The ultramontane opinion of the late King was not to the taste of the new Regent. Recoiling from the orthodoxy and Jesuit domination of his great uncle, the Regent embarked on a new course. By receiving Cardinal Noailles and exiling the former confessor, he gave public sign of the new spirit. In December, 1715, he institutionalized it by creating a Council of Conscience, composed of Gallicans and presided over by Cardinal Noailles, who had not accepted the papal bull. The new council was to guide the official religious policy of the crown.

This allowed the Gallicans and Jansenists to breathe. A clear minority of the laity and a tiny fraction of the clergy, the dissidents could hardly hope for royal support against the Pope. The Regent's sympathies did not extend to this, which could only mean an open and painful break with Rome. Moderate toleration was the most he

[3] "Minutes du conseil secret de Parlement de Paris," A.N., série X (1B) 8896, February 14, 1714.

intended. So the Gallicans and Jansenists were thrown on their own resources, with the assurance that the powers of the crown would not be turned against them. Their weapons were few. They could proceed by propaganda, by publishing their views in polemics and hoping to convert. This they did, aiming their shafts at the unpopular Society of Jesus, but these methods seemed only to impress people who were already Jansenist or Gallican. They could sue their opponents in the friendly Parlement of Paris, for the Gallican magistrates could be counted on for a favorable verdict. This too they did, and by this route of judicial appeal the Parlement was involved in the religious controversy.

A predisposition toward Jansenism and the Gallican liberties was family tradition with many of the magistrates of the Parlement. Father Pucelle, a nephew of Marshal Catinat and a councilor-clerk of the *Grand' Chambre,* was one of the leading Jansenists of France. Father Menguy, also a councilor in the *Grand' Chambre,* though somewhat more moderate, echoed his opinions. Among the *gens du Roi,* Aguesseau and Joly de Fleury were ardent Gallicans. Indeed, in the entire Parlement, only First President de Mesmes, Councilor Bragelogne, and President of Inquests Cochet de Saint-Vallier could be considered staunch ultramontanes, dependable supporters of Louis XIV's religious policies. All the rest leaned toward the Gallicans and were suspicious of the Papacy.

In addition to family tradition, however, there were substantive reasons for the magistrates' interest in the emerging religious controversies. An ultramontane policy of submission to the Pope had become identified with the Jesuits and with the centralization and absolutism of Louis XIV, both unpopular during the early Regency. Having suffered under the Sun King, the magistrates were not anxious to defend him at the cost of the esteem of the people. Furthermore, the magistrates thought of the Gallican liberties, which dated from the Pragmatic Sanction of Bourges of 1438 and the Concordat of Bologna of 1516, as part of the fundamental law of France. It was their duty to defend them. The Gallican liberties, like most French law, were indistinct enough in practice to be the source of lawsuits, out of which the magistrates made their living. In every way, a Gallican stand could only benefit the court—adding to its popular favor, giving weight to its dealings with the Regent, and increasing its case load. The magistrates confidently awaited the popular reaction to the ultramontanism of the previous reign.

They did not have long to wait. Curiously, the ultramontane majority which had accepted the papal bull eschewed caution and struck first. During the early months of 1716 a series of ultramontane pamphlets called Tocsins appeared in Paris.[4] They attacked the Sorbonne, which had not accepted *Unigenitus,* the Parlement of Paris, and worst of all flayed the Gallican liberties themselves. The first Tocsin appeared in March, the second soon afterward. Both were popularly attributed to the Jesuits, in particular to Father le Tellier. Both urged the episcopacy of France to unite with the papal nuncio to gain total acceptance of the bull.[5]

Widely distributed, and written in the ferocious style

[4] The nine Tocsins and their replies were collected in *Les Tocsins avec les écrits et les arrêts publiés contre ces libelles violentes et séditieux avec un recueil des mandements et autres pièces qui ont rapport aux écrits précédents* (n.p., 1716).

[5] J. Carreyre, *Le Jansénisme durant la Régence* (Louvain, 1929–33), I, 59–61; Villefore de Bourgoin, *Anecdotes ou Mémoires secrètes sur la Constitution "Unigenitus"* (Utrecht, 1734), II, 64–65.

common to religious polemics, the Tocsins soon gained considerable notoriety. The magistrates of the Parlement were disturbed. The Regent's frowns had not discouraged the Jesuits. The Parlement wasted no time in moving against this new menace. On April 4, Joly de Fleury, the senior advocate-general, denounced the Tocsins to the court, maintaining that they were tremendous libels and contrary to the established and fundamental laws of Church and state. On each line the Tocsins promoted schism and sedition. At a time when the Regent was working for clerical peace, these polemics urged bishops to conspire with the ambassador of a foreign power. Such activity violated the laws and customs of France, for bishops were not allowed to communicate with the nuncio without the permission of the King. Joly de Fleury asked for suppression, and the Parlement followed this advice. It ordered the Tocsins suppressed and forbade their publication or sale.[6]

The expected judicial condemnation did not stop the anonymous authors of the Tocsins. The Paris police were unable to prevent the printing and distribution of such pamphlets no matter what the Parlement ordered. Few were surprised to see more Tocsins. In April the fifth one appeared, carrying a blistering attack on the Sorbonne for its stand against the papal bull. It was supported by the Bishop of Toulon, who published a mandate attacking the Sorbonne and followed up on April 15 with a declaration

---

[6] Villefore, *Anecdotes ou Mémoires secrètes*, II, 65; Dorsanne, *Journal de la Constitution "Unigenitus,"* I, 262; Dangeau, *Journal*, XVI, 357; "Arrest de la Cour de Parlement portant suppression d'une Libelle intitulé 'Mémoire pour le corps des Pasteurs qui ont reçu la Constitution,'" B.N., série F 23672, April 4, 1716; "Registres du conseil secret de Parlement de Paris," A.N., série X (1A) 8432, fols. 197–201, April 4, 1716; "Minutes du conseil secret de Parlement de Paris," A.N., série X (1B) 8898, items 9–10, April 4, 1716.

expanding his acceptance of *Unigenitus*. All this was too much for the Gallican Cardinal Noailles. Unaccountably on the defensive during a regime friendly to his cause, the cardinal went to the Regent and demanded justice. The Regent sent the three pamphlets to the *gens du Roi*. The Parlement considered this new ultramontane outrage on May 11. Joly de Fleury repeated his previous condemnation of the Tocsins as libels against the peace of the Church. They injured the Gallican liberties by claiming the papal bull as a rule of faith and by taxing with heresy those bishops, and the theological faculty of the Sorbonne, who had not accepted it. Finally, the three pamphlets showed the same errors, the same strident spirit of argument, the same attitude of sedition as did the first Tocsins, which had been condemned in April. He demanded suppression. In a short and formal debate, the court suppressed the three tracts, forbidding their sale, printing, or distribution.[7]

Although Tocsins continued to appear from time to time throughout 1716, the Parlement of Paris took no further notice of them. Their novelty wore off, and their impact diminished. Further, a more important suit attracted the magistrates' attention. In April, 1715, before the death of Louis XIV had made such activities ill-advised, Bishop Mailly, Cardinal-Archbishop of Rheims, published a command that all clerics in his archdiocese

[7] Dangeau, *Journal*, XVI, 370; Dorsanne, *Journal de la Constitution "Unigenitus,"* I, 363–64; Villefore, *Anecdotes ou Mémoires secrètes*, II, 65–66, which is a direct copy from Dorsanne, *Journal de la Constitution "Unigenitus,"* I, 268; "Registres du conseil secret de Parlement de Paris," A.N., série X (1A) 8432, fols. 246–52, May 11, 1716; "Minutes du conseil secret de Parlement de Paris," A.N., série X (1B) 8898, items 7–8, May 11, 1716; "Arrest de la Cour de Parlement portant suppression d'une Libelle intitulé 'Lettre d'un Evesque à un Evesque' et autres imprimez," B.N., série F 23672, May 11, 1716.

accept the bull *Unigenitus*. The archbishop was an im-
placable, though not too effective, foe of the Gallicans
and Jansenists, and had issued his command as a matter
of routine submission to authority, both royal and ecclesiastical. Total submission was not forthcoming. Three
priests and three canons of the cathedral chapter at
Rheims refused to obey. They were excommunicated.[8]
After the death of the Sun King, the six recalcitrant clerics
obtained an order in council giving them the right to appeal to the Parlement by writ of error. On April 23, 1716,
the case was begun before a Gallican court, and followed
closely by a large audience of Parisians.

M. Chevalier, the lawyer for the three canons, opened
his plea with a profession of faith, to protect himself
against ecclesiastical censure for dealing with excommunicated men. Then he began, saying that the arch-
episcopal decree of excommunication was illegal in form
and content. As to form, the canons were not given a
chance to defend themselves; as to content, judgments
of bishops were not laws of the church, and there could
be no excommunication because of them. The Archbishop's decree should be struck down. Chevalier's pre-
sentation was popularly regarded as masterful, and loudly
applauded. M. Fessart, the lawyer for the Archbishop of
Rheims, said that his client, a peer of France, had the utmost respect for the Parlement, of which he was a member. Submission had not been demanded to the papal bull
as an article of faith, but only out of respect to the archbishop, the Pope, and the King. The decree was reasonable
and should be sustained.[9]

---

[8] Carreyre, *Le Jansénisme*, I, 52.

[9] Buvat, *Journal de la Régence*, I, 118–19, 139–40; Dorsanne, *Journal de la Constitution "Unigenitus,"* I, 265–67.

The hearings lasted through nine well-attended sessions, and the case was not decided until May 28. Then Joly de Fleury made his recommendations to the court. Never was an episcopal decree so full of error as this one from the Archbishop of Rheims. It required submission to the bull as an article of faith, and archbishops had no authority to do this. The decree should be annulled as abusive and erroneous. Although Fessart had presented an excellent case for the archbishop, the magistrates were not convinced. Joly de Fleury's advice was accepted, and Archbishop Mailly lost his decree and was assessed the costs of the case.[10]

This was no ordinary lawsuit. Archbishop Mailly was a cardinal, held the most important and privileged see in France, and was one of the leading ultramontanes of the realm. His conviction created great bitterness among his party. The papal nuncio intervened, appealing to the Regent to quash the case, as the canons and priests were showing no respect for the Pope.[11] This was also a crucial test case. Because the canons and priests won, no bishop could force acceptance of *Unigenitus* in his diocese. As soon as the decision against the archbishop was read, the great crowd of spectators in the foyer of the *Grand' Chambre* broke into loud applause.[12] The Parisian groundlings were raucously Gallican. Moreover, the

[10] Buvat, *Journal de la Régence*, I, 142; Dorsanne, *Journal de la Constitution "Unigenitus,"* I, 267; Dangeau, *Journal*, XVI, 385; "Arrest de la Cour de Parlement qui fait défense à tous les Archevesques et Evesques d'introduire dans leur Dioceses l'usage des souscriptions et signatures sans délibération des Evesques, revêtue des Lettres Patentes du Roy registrées en la Cour," B.N., série F 23672, May 28, 1716; "Registres des plaidories de Parlement de Paris," A.N., série X (1A) 6952, fols. 1–4, May 28, 1716.

[11] E. de Barthelémy (ed.), *Gazette de la Régence* (Paris, 1887), 80.

[12] Dorsanne, *Journal de la Constitution "Unigenitus,"* I, 267.

mere fact that the case had proceeded to its conclusion indicated the opinions of the Regent. Finally, it would now be possible for the hidden Gallicans and Jansenists among the lower clergy to make their opinions known without fear of excommunication by their bishop. The Pope and his bull were being badly dealt with in France.

For the Archbishop of Rheims this was not the end of the case. A year later he was still thinking about his priests and canons, and about punishing them. On March 20, 1717, he issued a mandate which excommunicated all clerics who did not accept *Unigenitus* within fifteen days.[13] This was appealed to the Parlement by writ of error, just as before.

When the case reached the Parlement a second time, the result was a foregone conclusion. The junior advocate-general Lamoignon de Blancmesnil brought in the advice of the *gens du Roi*. In a closed session he maintained that the Archbishop of Rheims was again treating the bull as an article of faith and injuring many of his best clergy. Moreover, he had insulted the Parlement, of which he was a member, by renewing his threat of excommunication. The First President then asked for the opinions of the magistrates. President Menars demanded that the archbishop pay damages to the priests and canons, and that an order be issued forbidding bishops to take any action against a refusal to accept the constitution *Unigenitus*. Father Pucelle, a violent Jansenist, strongly supported this position, saying that it was an affair of honor for the Parlement. The rest of the magistrates were not prepared to go this far, as it would probably offend the Regent, but the Parlement did issue an order condemning the Archbishop of Rheims in his case

[13] Buvat, *Journal de la Régence*, I, 263.

against the priests and canons.[14] Here the case ended, with the Archbishop of Rheims accepting the fact that on an appeal to the Parlement concerning *Unigenitus* he would be beaten. Yet he had not really lost much. Although the case ended with a formal victory for the six canons and priests, Archbishop Mailly had no difficulty in getting the rest of his clergy to accept the papal constitution. There were no more appeals.

As a result of the Tocsins and the case of the Archbishop of Rheims, the attitude of the magistrates of the Parlement on the Gallican liberties was quite clear. It was unlikely that a papal pamphlet would pass unnoticed, or that an ultramontane case could be won. Thus the judicial involvement of the court with the clerical quarrel began to diminish, and it would be a year before the Parlement would suppress another anti-Gallican tract.[15] But the Parlement was also a political organization, a fact that the Regent, in his efforts to win some sort of clerical peace, decided to exploit. In order to work out a religious solution in France without pressure from Rome, the Regent reverted to the methods

[14] Dangeau, *Journal*, XVIII, 97; Dorsanne, *Journal de la Constitution "Unigenitus,"* I, 340; Villefore, *Anecdotes ou Mémoires secrètes*, II, 215–16; "Registres des plaidories de Parlement de Paris," A.N., série X (1A) 6968, fols. 182–89, May 28, 1717.

[15] In connection with the second appeal against the Archbishop of Rheims a little pamphlet literature appeared. Two were suppressed by the Parlement in April, 1717. "Arrest de la Cour de Parlement portant suppression de deux écrits, le premier intitulé 'Lettre d'un Curé de Diocese de Chalons à un Curé de Rheims', du 20 février 1717; le second intitulé 'Sentance du Baillage de Chalons portant défense d'exposer en vente une Libelle intitulé Lettre d'un Curé du Diocese de Chalons à un Curé de Rheims,'" B.N., série F 23672, April 12, 1717; "Registres du conseil secret de Parlement de Paris," A.N., série X (1A) 8433, fols. 152–54, April 12, 1717; "Minutes du conseil secret de Parlement de Paris," A.N., série X (1B) 8898, item 13, April 12, 1717.

of Louis XIV. On December 12, 1716, he had Abbot Maupeou, a member of a magisterial family, write a circular letter to all the bishops of France, forbidding them to communicate with the Pope without the permission of the King.[16] This attempt to reinforce the isolation of the French clergy from Rome was then taken to the Parlement for a further measure of ratification. Always suspicious of the Pope, the magistrates were happy to issue an order supporting the Regent's letter.[17]

With his letter the Regent hoped to gain a breathing spell in order to end the split in the French Church. He did not succeed. Although communication with Rome was restricted, it could not be totally eliminated, and pressure for acceptance of the papal bull continued. The basic organizational structure of the Church, with the immense papal resources of confirmation and patronage, could hardly be overcome by a letter from Abbot Maupeou. Nor was the Regent or the Parlement able to alter the ratio of Gallicans to ultramontanes within the French Church. Although fairly numerous among the lower orders of the clergy, even here the Gallicans were, by no

[16] Text of the letter is in Dorsanne, *Journal de la Constitution "Unigenitus,"* I, 306.

[17] "Registres du conseil secret de Parlement de Paris," A.N., série X (1A) 8433, fols. 26–27, December 16, 1716; "Minutes du conseil secret de Parlement de Paris," A.N., série X (1B) 8898, item 32, December 16, 1716. Buvat, *Journal de la Régence,* I, 237; Dorsanne, *Journal de la Constitution "Unigenitus,"* I, 307; Villefore, *Anecdotes ou Mémoires secrètes,* II, 138; Dangeau, *Journal,* XVI, 507; Guillaume de Lamoignon, "Journal historique de Guillaume de Lamoignon advocat-général du Parlement de Paris, 1713–1718," ed. Henri Courteault, *Annuaire-Bulletin de la Société de l'histoire de France,* XLVII (1910), 260; "Arrest de la Cour de Parlement qui renouvelle les défenses de recevoir, publier ou exécuter imprimer, vendre ou distribuer aucunes Bulles ou Brefs de la Cour de Rome sans Lettres Patentes du Roy registrées en ladite Cour," B.N., série F 23672, December 16, 1716.

stretch of the imagination, a majority. Gallican bishops, canons, abbots, and vicars-general were pitifully few, and the papal majority was far too great and determined to be coerced by the Parlement or replaced by the Regent. It was becoming obvious by 1717 that the rift could only be closed on papal terms, which meant the acceptance of *Unigenitus.*

The Gallican clergy were not ready for that. On March 1, 1717, at the University of Paris, the bishops of Senez, Boulogne, Montpellier, and Mirepoix signed an appeal from the Pope to a future general council of the Church on the question of the bull *Unigenitus.* On April 3, Cardinal Noailles added his appeal. The Gallican position was clearly staked out, and in a way that could hardly please the Pope, but no one rallied around the flag. No other episcopal appeals were added to the five already recorded, and the Gallican party remained a minority of five out of about 140 bishops.

The appeals to a future council by the cardinal and the four bishops clearly promised an increase in both the number and temper of the clerical polemics. While sympathetic to the Gallican position, which upheld the power of the crown, the Regent did not want a major ecclesiastical uproar. He moved immediately to forestall it. On April 10, during a Council of Regency, Chancellor Aguesseau was ordered to arrange a meeting on the papal bull, to see if the unhappy impact of the appeals at Rome could not be reduced.

The very next day the Regent received Aguesseau, the *gens du Roi,* First President de Mesmes, and some other advisors. A proposal was made that the Regent impose silence on all parties concerning the bull. Everyone had an opinion. The new procurer-general Joly de Fleury was the most ardent Gallican and said that he would defend the proposed declaration if it were based on the appeals to the future council. The First President merely wished to allow the Parlement to take the steps necessary to maintain public order. The advocate-general Lamoignon de Blancmesnil favored the declaration of silence; his new colleague, Chauvelin, wished to do nothing. No decision was reached, and the question was put off until April 18, when the group was to meet again.[18]

The next session was no more productive. The participants wandered from the subject and discussed the Archbishop of Rheims, whose case was then in its second round before the Parlement. They agreed not to interfere. Penalties against the sale of contraband books were increased, although they were already so severe as to be impossible to enforce.[19] The Regent and his advisors were as quick to contemplate solutions as they were slow to execute them.

Yet the proposed declaration of silence concerning *Unigenitus* was not forgotten. The Regent toyed with the idea the entire summer. Finally, toward the end of September, he had the chancellor and Marshal Huxelles draw up a draft of an edict imposing silence on all factions ". . . during the term of the negotiations with Rome . . .," negotiations which had not really been opened.[20] On October 1, Aguesseau showed his draft to the Regent, who liked it, and asked the approval of the Gallican Cardinal Noailles. From him the proposed decla-

---

[18] Lamoignon, "Journal historique," 271–80, gives a long and detailed description of the meeting. See also Dorsanne, *Journal de la Constitution "Unigenitus,"* I, 330–31; Villefore, *Anecdotes ou Mémoires sècretes,* II, 217.

[19] Lamoignon, "Journal historique," 280–81.

[20] Dorsanne, *Journal de la Constitution "Unigenitus,"* I, 353–54.

ration went to the *gens du Roi* and the First President, who advised that it be sent to the Parlement for registration. Again the Regent used the political power and prestige of his Parlement and sent his declaration in, feeling that the Gallicans would respect a magisterial pronouncement and obey the law. On October 8 the *gens du Roi* brought the declaration to the court. It was immediately registered without discussion, and the First President was instructed to tell the Regent that the bishops must be forbidden to assemble to discuss the new law.[21]

The Regent clearly hoped that his declaration of silence would give him time to negotiate the whole matter with Rome. It should cut down somewhat the number of clerical polemics in France. The declaration should give the government time to catch its breath and think things over. But it did not. No one was satisfied. Both sides felt they had something to say and were determined to say it. The Gallicans saw themselves as a beleaguered minority, which could not triumph unless free to convert at least the uncommitted. The ultramontanes were greatly irritated at a declaration that kept them from the pious work of unmasking Jansenist schismatics. The declaration gravely underestimated clerical tenacity on doctrine and the compulsion to publish. The Regent's law was soon ignored.

The first major rupture of the declaration of silence

[21] *Ibid.*, I, 354–56; Dangeau, *Journal*, XVII, 170–71; Villefore, *Anecdotes ou Mémoires secrètes*, II, 244; "Registres du conseil secret du Parlement de Paris," A.N., série X (1A) 8433, fol. 453, October 8, 1717; "Minutes du conseil secret de Parlement de Paris," A.N., série X (1B) 8898, item 5, October 8, 1717; "Déclaration du Roy qui suspend toutes les disputes, contestations, et differends formez dans le Royaume à l'occasion de la Constitution de Nostre Saint Père le Pape, contre le Livre des 'Réflexions morales sur le Nouveau Testament,'" B.N., série F 23621 (819), October, 1717.

was sensational, for it involved Cardinal Noailles, the most prominent Gallican and Jansenist in the world. Although the cardinal had appealed to a future general council against the bull, his appeal had not been published. Late in November, 1717, however, a great many printed copies of this appeal were circulated in Paris.[22] The cardinal was horrified and maintained that they had appeared without his knowledge or approval. Were the appeal to be condemned to suppression, which was quite certain, it would be a blow to the Gallican party, and to the dignity of the cardinal. He rushed to see the Regent, claiming that he was a victim of a conspiracy, asserting that *agents provocateurs* were at work, and disavowing the printing of the appeal.[23] A letter and a memoir, both sent to the Regent, followed. He again claimed that the appeal had been published without his knowledge. While he did desire its suppression, he did not want the appeal itself attacked. The appeal was valuable and good, and its publication was a trick to embarrass him.[24] As a final measure of insurance, he sent the Regent an additional memorandum which he wanted passed on to the *gens du Roi*. Here again the agitated cardinal disavowed the publication of his appeal while upholding its content. He sent this memorandum also to the First President.[25]

[22] "Acte d'appel de Monseigneur le Cardinal de Noailles, Archévêque de Paris, de 3 avril 1717 au Pape mieux conseillé et au futur concile générale, de Constitution 'Unigenitus' du 8 septembre 1713 et de tout qui s'en ensuivi et pourra ensuivre," in *Les Tocsins*; Dorsanne, *Journal de la Constitution "Unigenitus,"* I, 376; Buvat, *Journal de la Régence*, I, 309; Villefore, *Anecdotes ou Mémoires secrètes*, II, 269–70.

[23] Dorsanne, *Journal de la Constitution "Unigenitus,"* I, 376–77; Villefore, *Anecdotes ou Mémoires secrètes*, II, 270.

[24] Dorsanne, *Journal de la Constitution "Unigenitus,"* I, 377. Text of the letter is in Villefore, *Anecdotes ou Mémoires secrètes*, II, 270–72.

[25] Dorsanne, *Journal de la Constitution "Unigenitus,"* I, 377–78. Text

During the last days of November the magistrates argued over the coming suppression of the cardinal's appeal by the Parlement. No one doubted that the Parlement, in order to maintain any reputation for honor and justice, would have to act against the appeal. Some, like the First President and the chancellor, wished to attack the appeal itself and humiliate the cardinal; others, like Joly de Fleury, wished to attack only its publication. The latter was the majority view.

On December 1 the Parlement met to consider Cardinal Noailles' appeal. Advocate-General Lamoignon de Blancmesnil said that the people saw with grief the printing of the cardinal's appeal without his knowledge or permission. This could only be the work of seditious spirits who wished to cause schism in the Church, while the cardinal himself worked for peace. Therefore, in view of all this and of the declaration of silence of October, the *gens du Roi* were obliged to ask for suppression.

Although they hated to do it, the magistrates could see no alternative to the suppression of the cardinal's appeal. The session proceeded smoothly enough, though without enthusiasm, until Father Pucelle, one of the leading Jansenists of France, spoke. He suspected that the distinction between the appeal and the fact of its publication was becoming blurred. Strongly in favor of the appeal, he maintained that Rome would interpret suppression to include the nature of the appeal itself. He demanded that the order of suppression state specifically that it was without prejudice to the appeal and applied only to its publication. De Mesmes interrupted, saying that the whole affair had been arranged with the *gens du Roi* and

of the declaration is in Villefore, *Anecdotes ou Mémoires secrètes*, II, 277–80.

the cardinal himself and was settled. It was. Only Croiset agreed with Father Pucelle. The rest of the magistrates voted for the suppression demanded by the advocate-general.[26]

The publication of Cardinal Noailles' appeal was an international event. In Rome it was regarded as a clear affront to the Pope, and the Parlement's condemnation was insufficient. The Pope decided to attack the cardinal's appeal himself and state clearly to the Church his displeasure with refusals to accept papal bulls. The actual condemnation was made by the Inquisition. On February 16, 1718, the Holy Office passed a decree strongly condemning the appeals of the four bishops and Cardinal Noailles against the bull *Unigenitus*.

This was not calculated as a diplomatic gesture. It was designed to increase the pressure on the Regent. The Regent saw it was an extremely unwelcome intrusion into the religious politics of France, a serious blow to the clerical peace and quiet he was striving for. The cardinal and his Gallicans were naturally horrified. The Parlement rushed to attack the Roman enemy. On March 28, soon after the decree had reached France, the *gens du Roi* brought it to the Parlement. The magistrates were told that it attacked the Gallican liberties, one of which was the right of appeal to a Church council. It hindered the Regent in his quest for peace. It should be

[26] "Arrest de la Cour de Parlement du décembre 1, 1717 qui ordonne l'exécution de la Déclaration du septième octobre dernier," B.N., série F 23672, December 1, 1717; Buvat, *Journal de la Régence*, I, 309–10; Villefore, *Anecdotes ou Mémoires secrètes*, II, 282; Dangeau, *Journal*, XVII, 203–204; Dorsanne, *Journal de la Constitution "Unigenitus,"* I, 378–79; "Registres du conseil secret de Parlement de Paris," A.N., série X (1A) 8434, fols. 6–8, December 1, 1717; "Minutes du conseil secret de Parlement de Paris," A.N., série X (1B) 8899, item 1, December 1, 1717.

suppressed. The magistrates needed no special urging and condemned the decree of the Inquisition the same day they considered it.[27] This ended the matter, for the Papacy did not intend to play games with the Parlement of Paris. The papal position had been stated. Time and slow, inexorable pressure from the Church would insure complete submission. The Parlement thought in years, the Pope in centuries. He had only to wait.

But the Parlement and the Gallicans could not wait. Already a minority, enjoying royal support that might end any time, the Gallicans and Jansenists desperately needed a rapid victory over the Pope and his bull. Using the certain support of the magistrates of the Parlement, the Gallicans had attacked ultramontane pamphlets and attempts to enforce acceptance of *Unigenitus*. In every case they had been victorious. Yet the Gallicans were not noticeably stronger in 1718 than they had been in 1715. Royal support and the Parlement had availed than nothing. The Parlement had been unable to convert France to the Gallican view, had not appreciably reduced ultramontane literature, and could render only the most tentative protection to the beleaguered Gallicans among the lower clergy. Insofar as they were aimed at promoting the Gallican cause, the activities of the Parlement had failed. The Regent's friendship had meant much more. But even the Regent would not break with Rome

[27] "Registres du conseil secret de Parlement de Paris," A.N., série X (1A) 8434, fols. 244–46, March 28, 1718; "Minutes du conseil secret de Parlement de Paris," A.N., série X (1B) 8899, item 58, March 28, 1718; "Arrest de la Cour de Parlement qui ordonne la saisie et la suppression d'un Décret de l'Inquisition portant condemnation de l'Ecrit intitulé 'Acte d'appel interjetté le premier Mars 1717 etc.,' et de celui intitulé 'Acte d'appel de son Eminence Monseigneur le Cardinal de Noailles etc.,' et qui ordonne l'exécution de la Déclaration du septième Octobre dernier," B.N., série F 23672, March 28, 1718.

over a theoretical threat to the Gallican liberties. As long as he retained control over the Church benefices, he was satisfied.

For its part, the Parlement had done more than defend a particular view of Church organization. It had staked out a political position, one which the magistrates would maintain throughout the entire century and which would culminate in the expulsion of the Jesuits from France. It seems clear that the magistrates fervently believed in the Gallican liberties, and in the evil intentions of the Pope. They were to suffer for this belief under Cardinal Fleury, and again in the 1750's. But the sincerity of the magistrates is not the issue—at this date it hardly matters —and it is only partially relevant that they chose to defend the Gallican, rather than the ultramontane, position. What is extraordinarily important is that the Parlement felt called upon to take any religious position, that the magistrates felt, and acted as if, religious affairs were their proper judicial and political sphere. The magistrates were obliged, considered it their clear and vital duty, to take a stand on the question Gallican or ultramontane. That they were Gallican was an accident of history. That they felt compelled to take a political position on religion and the Church was explicit in their attitudes toward what they regarded as the constitution of France.

CHAPTER IV

The Royal Finances 1715–18

AT THE TIME of Louis XIV's death, the plight of his treasury surpassed all ordinary considerations. Although some progress had been made since 1713 to liquidate the fiscal morass of the Spanish Succession, two years was too short a time in which to reconstruct the finances. Trade was stagnant, taxes were maladministered, a huge annual deficit still continued, and larger new loans were inevitable. The Regent fell heir to this, and his most immediate problem was to bring some kind of order out of the financial chaos.

The Regent's new advisors found the treasury ruined. The royal debt stood at nearly two billion *livres*, not including over six hundred million in short-term, unfunded government paper.[1] Income for 1721 had been anticipated and spent, and a start was about to be made on the income for 1722. Revenues for 1715 were about 69 million *livres*, but expenditures were 146 million. Debt service alone, if met, would run over 86 million.[2] Not only was there debt

[1] Warren Scoville, *The Persecution of Huguenots and French Economic Development, 1680-1720* (Berkeley, 1960), 205; Earl Hamilton, "Origin and Growth of the National Debt in Western Europe," *American Economic Review, Proceedings,* XXXVII (1947), 118–40.

[2] "Mémoire du duc de Noailles sur les finances," Manuscrits français, B.N., No. 11152, fols. 1–134, June 19–26, 1717; Marcel Marion, *Histoire financière de la France depuis 1715* (Paris, 1914–31), I, 61–65. Every-

71

and a deficit; the means of rectifying the fiscal disorder were lacking. The system of taxation was only beginning to function normally after the dislocations of war. From 1709 to 1714 the indirect taxes had not been farmed. Yields were so poor and expenses so high that it cost more to collect the *aides* and *gabelles* than they were worth. Not until 1714, with the Nerville Lease, could the crown induce the farmers-general to collect the indirect taxes, and even then the royal income was lower than it had been since the 1670's.[3] The *taille* and other direct taxes were in a similar condition, with receipts down and the peasants generally unable to pay. The credit of the state was attacked from both flanks—on the one side by the huge debt, and on the other by a deficit resulting from the inability to tax.

The new Regent was expected to take energetic steps toward solving the fiscal crisis. The Duke of Saint-Simon advised bankruptcy and an Estates-General. The Duke of Noailles, appointed to chair the Council of Finances, had a more conservative solution, partial repudiation and a Chamber of Justice to tax the rich.[4] John Law claimed that his scheme for a royal bank of issue would restore the King's credit, and eventually even pay the national debt. The magistrates of the Parlement, with their tradi-

one gives different figures for the exact fiscal state of the crown in 1715. Here I have used those of the Duke of Noailles, not because they are more accurate than those of Marion or others—they probably are not —but because they represent the opinions of the man charged with solving the problem.

[3] Marion, *Histoire financière*, I, 70–72; George T. Matthews, *The Royal General Farms in Eighteenth Century France* (New York, 1958), 58–61; François Veron de Forbonnais, *Recherches et considérations sur les finances de France depuis l'année 1559 jusqu'à l'année 1721* (Basle, 1758), II, 220.

[4] Dangeau, *Journal*, XVI, 320.

tional views on the royal fisc, favored the Duke of Noailles' advice and expected immediate retrenchments in the expenditures of the crown.

One of the Regent's first edicts, therefore, produced surprise and dismay within the Parlement. On September 22, 1715, the Regent created the office of Superintendent of the Postal Service of France and gave it to Colbert de Torcy as compensation for the suppression of his former office of Secretary of State, which had cost 800,000 *livres*.[5] This could hardly be called a step in the right direction. It established a new office which would inevitably be a burden on the finances. True retrenchment would have been abolition of Colbert de Torcy's office without compensation, as the former minister was wealthy enough to afford it.

The edict was sent to the Interim Chamber of the Parlement for registration. The magistrates were still favorable to the Regent, and decided to register the edict, with the stipulation that such registration be provisional until the full company had a chance to agree to it.[6] On February 8, 1716, the entire corps of magistrates considered it, along with an edict of January establishing the office of Superintendent of the Buildings of the King. The magistrates registered neither, but named Le Nain and Musnier as commissioners to study the two documents.[7]

[5] *Ibid.*, XVI, 196; Villars, *Mémoires*, IV, 75, Flammermont (ed.), *Les Remontrances*, I, 42; Saint-Simon, *Mémoires*, XXIX, 86, 122; "Edit du Roy portant création de la charge de Grand-Maistre et Surintendant-Général des Postes, Courriers et Relais de France et d'autre charges subalternes pour le service des postes," B.N., série F 23621 (152), September, 1715.

[6] Flammermont (ed.), *Les Remontrances*, I, 43; "Minutes du conseil secret de Parlement de Paris," A.N., série X (1B) 8897, items 1–2, October 1, 1715.

[7] Flammermont (ed.), *Les Remontrances*, I, 43; Dangeau, *Journal*,

The commissioners were in no hurry to report. Not until April 24 did they bring the two edicts to the floor of the Parlement. In his recommendation Le Nain said that the offices of Superintendent of the Postal Service and Superintendent of the Buildings had at one time been suppressed, with clauses forbidding their re-establishment, and therefore ought to remain suppressed. The magistrates could hardly reject the advice of the commission, particularly as the dean of the *Grand' Chambre*, Le Nain, was its reporter. The vote to send a remonstrance to the King on the edicts was a landslide, 85 to 25, and the protest was set for May 13.[8]

The remonstrance was extremely short and concise, particularly remarkable considering the verbosity common in eighteenth-century official prose. The document began by assuring the King that the Parlement had every confidence in the men chosen for the offices created by the two edicts. But it was not a question of the men; the offices themselves were undesirable. The position of Superintendent of the Posts was unnecessary, even contrary to the interests of the state. Louis XIV had seen this and had suppressed the office in 1692. By that act of suppression the office was never to be re-established. Furthermore, the office would be a drain on the treasury at a time when the crown was in desperate straits and the whole nation was contributing to assist the Regent in saving the treasury. The magistrates of the sovereign courts had taken a reduction in salary, and a similar retrenchment ought to be applied in the present case. The

---

XVI, 317–18; Villars, *Mémoires*, IV, 75; "Edit du Roy portant création de la charge de Surintendent et Ordinateur-Général des Bâtimens du Roy," B.N., série F 23621 (243), January, 1716.

[8] Dangeau, *Journal*, XVI, 386; Saint-Simon, *Mémoires*, XXX, 86; Flammermont (ed.), *Les Remontrances*, I, 42.

arguments against the office of Superintendent of the Buildings were the same. This position too had been abolished by the late King, never to be re-established, and the loss to the treasury was the same. The people hoped the Regent could do the work of the offices himself, for they had great confidence in his abilities. The remonstrance closed with the statement that the Parlement was certain that the Regent would take its protest in good faith, as it had been submitted for the good of the people as proof of the court's devotion and zeal, and with all confidence in the judgment and justice of the crown.[9]

The remonstrance was an effective document. It struck the Regent at his weakest point, extravagance. A generous man, he could not break away from the Sun King's pattern of distributing offices and pensions to the courtiers who surrounded and supported him. He had broken up the royal court by moving from Versailles to Paris, but he was unable to bankrupt the aristocratic courtiers who depended on the King for their fortunes and careers. The crown's obligation to support its nobility would be unchanged during the Regency. But in this case, the Regent was embarrassed. He had set a bad example. He seemed to encourage pensions as usual. When all agreed that the most severe retrenchments and the greatest efforts ought to be made to sustain the royal credit, he had proposed to spend money unnecessarily. That the fallen minister deserved the money no one denied, but the time for sacrifices had come. The short-term debt had just been reduced 60 per cent, and the *rentes* funded at great loss to their holders. Even the magistrates had given. The Regent's moral position on the two edicts was weak, and he knew it.

[9] Text is in Flammermont (ed.), *Les Remontrances*, I, 42–46.

When negotiations with the Parlement were opened, the magistrates, strong in the righteousness of fiscal responsibility, were not at all ready to register the edicts, even with modifications. On July 13, when the court assembled to hear the reply to the remonstrance, the edicts still had not been registered. The First President's news that the Regent wished registration was greeted with the fact that the magistrates did not.[10] As the summer drifted on, amid the alarms and excesses of the Chamber of Justice, with all attention riveted on the finances, the Regent decided to make concessions. On August 28 he sent the Parlement two interpretative declarations which modified the edicts somewhat as the court wished.[11] These were remanded to a commission to be studied, but the report of the commission was against registration. The full court again upheld its commissioners and decided on new remonstrances.[12]

When he learned of this, the Regent decided that the time had come to act. Though small in themselves, the two edicts had become a symbol of royal authority, and the Regent had not enjoyed that authority long enough to be careless of it. On September 7, the last day of the full session of the Parlement, he sent Marquis Effiat to the court with a further interpretation of the edict on the

[10] "Registres du conseil secret de Parlement de Paris," A.N., série X (1A) 8432, fol. 434, July 15, 1716; "Minutes du conseil secret de Parlement de Paris," A.N., série X (1B) 8898, item 13, July 13, 1716; Dangeau, *Journal*, XVI, 412–13.

[11] "Déclaration du Roy en interpretation de l'Edit de création de la charge de Grand-Maistre et Surintendant-General des Postes," B.N., série F 23621 (503), August 28, 1716; "Déclaration du Roy en interpretation de l'Edit de création de la charge de Surintendant-General des Bâtimens du Roy," B.N., série F 23621 (242), August 28, 1716.

[12] "Registres du conseil secret de Parlement de Paris," A.N., série X (1A) 8432, fols. 405–406, September 5, 1716.

buildings.[13] The marquis was conducted to the *Grand'*
Chambre, where he presented the First President with a
lettre de cachet from the Regent which ordered registration. He then spoke to the magistrates. Since the Regent
had favorably received the remonstrance, he had hoped
that the Parlement would favorably receive the interpretative declarations of August 28. But it had not, and the
Regent was now obliged to use his authority. The edicts
must be registered immediately. The First President
asked the opinions of the magistrates. Faced with the
Regent's determination, and appeased with a further modification of the edict on the buildings, the Parlement registered the two edicts, together with their interpretative
declarations. The sessions closed, and the vacations began at once.[14]

This was the first instance of opposition to a royal edict
in over forty years, and the court acquitted itself well and
honorably. Attacking the two edicts on the grounds of
the general good, rather than on the basis of particular
privilege, the magistrates had been able to wring concessions from the Regent. Although the forced registration
showed that the Regent could exercise power when he
chose to, the course of events from remonstrance to registration demonstrated his reluctance to use force in a
dubious cause. There seemed to be no doubt that the
political powers of the Parlement had been returned. The

[13] Dangeau, *Journal,* XVI, 449–50; "Déclaration du Roy en interpretation de celle d'aoust 28," B.N., série F 23621 (242), October 6, 1716.

[14] Text of the meeting is in Flammermont (ed.), *Les Remontrances,*
I, 46–49. See also Dangeau, *Journal,* XVI, 450; Buvat, *Journal de la*
Régence, I, 166; Saint-Simon, *Mémoires,* XXX, 210; "Registres du
conseil secret de Parlement de Paris," A.N., série X (1A) 8432, fols. 428–
29, September 7, 1716; "Minutes du conseil secret de Parlement de
Paris," A.N., série X (1B) 8898, item 17, September 7, 1716.

court's action in suppressing the Tocsins and condemning the Archbishop of Rheims, and its opposition to the Regent's edicts, could only encourage the magistrates to expand their political activities in 1717. In reviewing their policies, the magistrates felt that they had both performed their duty and expanded the influence of the court.

Although the crown tried various expedients during 1716, the finances did not improve. A bureau of inquiry had indeed reduced the unfunded debt by 350 million *livres*, but the long-term royal debt was still untouched.[15] The Chamber of Justice proved a failure and brought in only 91 million, and that mostly in paper. Nor had the deficit been decreased. It seemed that a systematic survey of the fiscal confusion and a number of moderate and sensible remedies were needed. Therefore, the Duke of Noailles presented to the Council of Regency an exhaustive memoir on the general state of the finances and the steps necessary to improve it.[16] After studying the memoir, the Regent accepted its conclusions and began to prepare legislation embodying its recommendations. On August 26, 1717, the final drafts of the edicts were ready and were sent to the Parlement for registration.

The main edict was a long document of eighteen articles. Its preamble stated that the King wished only to ease the financial burdens of his subjects and to retrench royal expenses. The edict was to be a step in re-establishing order in the fisc. The *dixième*, established in 1710 as a war measure, was abolished. The loss in income would not be great, as most people with enough money to pay the tax had evaded it. But even so, any small reduction

[15] Matthews, *The Royal General Farms*, 60–61; Earl Hamilton, "Prices and Wages at Paris under John Law's System," *Quarterly Journal of Economics*, II (1936–37), 43–45.

[16] Text of the memoir is in Manuscrits français, B.N., No. 11152.

in income had to be made up, for the crown was operating at a deficit. Article three reduced pensions, and the fourth and fifth ones abolished free salt privileges and all other exemptions to the indirect taxes. The magistrates of the Parlement were among those who enjoyed the valuable privilege of free salt and the immunity from arbitrary search by the general farms which went with it. No little saving was overlooked. Even the expenses of cleaning the streets of Paris were transferred from the crown to the municipal government.

The edict also outlined the methods proposed for eliminating the rest of the bills of state, which formed the bulk of the short-term debt. Articles eleven and thirteen stated that these could be converted into annuities at 6 per cent, or be used to buy shares in John Law's new Company of the West, or be used to buy parts of the royal domain or a chance in the national lottery. As the bills stood at considerable discount, any of these options represented a way of getting some value for them and were a real bargain. If the outstanding bills were not converted by the new year, they would cease to draw interest and become totally worthless. The bills of the receivers-general of the finances, who collected the *taille*, were also mentioned. They had been drawing 7½ per cent interest, which the crown could not afford to pay. Nor could the King pay back the principal. Articles fourteen through eighteen converted the bills of the receivers-general into 4 per cent treasury notes, with the interest to be paid from the general funds and not by the receivers-general themselves.[17] These last five articles

[17] "Edit du Roy portant suppression du dixième du revenue des biens, règlement touchant les billets de l'Etat, ceux des receuveurs-généraux et les pensions," B.N., série F 23621 (783), August 26, 1717.

hit the purses of the magistrates hard, and complaint was likely. Along with this edict went several others. One which was of considerable importance established John Law's Company of the West, a second authorized sale of part of the royal domain, and a third established annuities to be bought with the bills of state. The last suppressed several offices which had drawn almost universal complaint.[18] A large package was sent to the Parlement, but none of the proposed legislation, except John Law's bank, touched on either the basic ills of the fiscal structure or any real measures for reform. The inequities in tax assessments between town and country and the various provinces were left untouched. The tax privileges of the nobles were still intact, and venality of office was not mentioned. The entire tax structure remained regressive, with taxes falling most heavily on those who were unable to pay. The Regent's edicts said nothing about all of this. The reform they promised was largely illusory. Only John Law's bank, providing sorely needed commercial credit at reasonable rates, promised any real benefit at all. Beyond that the Regent had only tinkered with the old machinery.

In spite of the innocuous nature of the Regent's proposals, the magistrates voiced serious misgivings. Over a hundred of them voted to name commissioners to ex-

[18] "Lettres patentes en forme d'Edit portant établissement d'une Compagnie de Commerce sous le nom de Compagnie d'Occident," B.N., série F 23621 (798), August 26, 1717; "Edit du Roy pour la vente et engagement des petits domaines," B.N., série F 23621 (786), August 26, 1717; "Edit du Roy portant création de 1.200.000 livres de rentes viagères pour parvenir a l'extension des billets de l'Etat et de la caisse commune des recettes générales," B.N., série F 23621 (788), August 26, 1717; "Edit du Roy portant suppression des offices de gouveneurs lieutenants du Roy et majors de ville creez par l'Edit d' aoust 1696 et décembre 1708," B.N., série F 23621 (797), August 26, 1717.

amine the edicts. This was the usual procedure, but the magistrates wanted more. The same majority asked the Regent for an abstract of the financial condition of the realm.[19] This was a most unusual step, for the finances of the kingdom were considered a state secret, and the Regent was certain to object to such a presumptuous request. Nonetheless, the First President delivered the message. The indignant Regent rejected it outright, snapping that he was unable to see how a cabal in the Parlement could delay benefits the King wished to give his subjects. De Mesmes reported to his company that the magistrates could not have the financial statement, for to divulge such information would be a diminution of royal authority.[20]

When de Mesmes made his report, there was considerable grumbling and discontent. The Regency was two years old, and fiscal problems were not noticeably closer to being solved than they had been under the Sun King. But nothing could be done about it, so a commission was named to examine the edicts. The commissioners worked for the first three days of September and reported to the Parlement on the fourth. As a result of their advice, the magistrates decided to register a part of the large edict. Articles one through five, seven through ten, and seventeen and eighteen were approved. These

[19] Dangeau, *Journal*, XVII, 154; Buvat, *Journal de la Régence*, I, 298; Marais, *Journal et Mémoires*, I, 230–31; Collection Delisle, A.N., série U 360, August 28, 1717; "Registres du conseil secret de Parlement de Paris," A.N., série X (1A) 8433, fol. 449; "Minutes du conseil secret de Parlement de Paris," A.N., série X (1B) 8899, item 47, August 28, 1717.

[20] Collection Delisle, A.N., série U 360, August 31, 1717; Barthelémy (ed.), *Gazette de la Régence*, September 9, 1717, pp. 201–202; "Registres du conseil secret de Parlement de Paris," A.N., série X (1A) 8433, fols. 449–51, August 31, 1717; "Minutes du conseil secret de Parlement de Paris," A.N., série X (1B) 8899, item 51, August 31, 1717.

suppressed the *dixième* and the exemptions to the salt tax, which the magistrates had to do or lose all public support. The rest of the edict, concerning the bills of state, those of the receivers-general, and the municipal expenses of Paris, was rejected. Of these articles, the magistrates merely said they would be further examined and registered, "if they ought to be. . . ." [21]

This procedure was unusual. According to the provisions of the Edict of 1673, still in effect, the Parlement had no right to register only part of an edict and to reject the rest. The magistrates were clearly exceeding the authority given them in the Declaration of Vincennes and issuing a challenge to the royal prerogative. The powers of the Parlement were being enlarged at the expense of the crown. Would the amiable Regent do anything about it? The magistrates thought not. It seemed like such a small matter that he would probably overlook it. But in the unwritten and infinitely elastic constitutional framework of Old Regime France, nothing was a small matter. The exact relationship of the various institutions to each other depended on their political strength at the moment. It was quite possible for the crown to lose much of its legislative power to the Parlement; it had done so in the Fronde and would do so again in the 1780's. Much that had once been considered contrary to the fundamental laws of France became acceptable by the prescriptive right of long usage. Most of the royal taxes fell into that category, and rejection of

[21] "Minutes du conseil secret de Parlement de Paris," A.N., série X (1B) 8899, item 7, September 4, 1717; Marais, *Journal et Mémoires*, I, 232; Flammermont (ed.), *Les Remontrances*, I, 50; Buvat, *Journal de la Régence*, I, 302–303; Dangeau, *Journal*, XVII, 157; Saint-Simon, *Mémoires*, XXXII, 106.

part of an edict by the Parlement might also. No law or immutable custom stood in the way, only the Regent's determination to resist. The magistrates could hope that this important increase in their powers would become permanent. In any case, however, they thought that the Regent would not object this time, and that they would have their way with his edict.

The Regent did take steps, but they did not deal with the constitutional challenge. He moved against the threat to his edicts, not to his powers. He concerned himself with the royal finances, not the royal prerogative. On September 5, the First President, the commissioners examining the edicts, the *gens du Roi,* and the chancellor were called to the Palais Royal to face the Regent and the Duke of Noailles. Distraught by the magistrates' opposition, the duke explained the necessity for the edicts. Assisted by John Law, he worked for over four hours, discussing the finances and the savings which the edicts would bring. The Regent himself said nothing. Showing considerable patience and self-control, he sat through the entire session. The Parlement's move to enlarge its political power and constitutional position passed without comment.[22]

When the court met on September 6, the First President told the magistrates of the discussion at the Palais Royal, adding that everyone had been very well received. The Parlement reconsidered the edicts and agreed to register all the short ones, and all the articles of the main bill except those pertaining to the bills of state, the receivers-general, and the municipal expenses of Paris. By a narrow

[22] Collection Delisle, A.N., série U 360, September 4, 1717; Marais, *Journal et Mémoires,* I, 233–35; Barthelémy (ed.), *Gazette de la Régence,* September 9, 1717, pp. 204–205.

margin, 81 to 73, a remonstrance was voted for those articles.[23]

This helped, but it did not satisfy the Regent. He had not sat through four hours of fiscal explanations for nothing. The articles concerning the bills of state and the receivers-general were important to his program, and he did not mean to let them go. Suspecting the Parlement of trying to delay registration until after the vacations began on September 7, he continued its sessions until September 14. The additional week should bring results.[24]

This extension of the sessions was not unwelcome to the magistrates. They were thinking of two things—their opposition to the edict and the extension of the political powers of the court. If the Regent were so anxious to have the Parlement's approval for his financial program, perhaps the court could obtain concessions everywhere. So the magistrates asked to present a remonstrance on the non-registered portions of the disputed edict. Should the Regent agree to receive such a document, he would implicitly recognize the right of the court to register only parts of an edict and reject, or at least modify, the rest. Hoping that by hearing the remonstrance he would get his edict registered, the Regent ignored the constitutional challenge and agreed to a remonstrance on September 9.

The protest began with a compliment to the Regent, thanking him for the abolition of the *dixième* and expressing the hope that the burdens of the people might

[23] "Registres du conseil secret de Parlement de Paris," A.N., série X (1A) 8433, fols. 421–22, September 6, 1717; "Minutes du conseil secret de Parlement de Paris," A.N., série X (1B) 8899, item 9, September 6, 1717; Marais, *Journal et Mémoires*, I, 235; Saint-Simon, *Mémoires*, XXXII, 398–99.

[24] "Registres du conseil secret de Parlement de Paris," A.N., série X (1A) 8433, fol. 421, September 6, 1717; Dangeau, *Journal*, XVII, 158.

be eased even more. To this end, and to aid in the processes of good government, the Parlement had gladly registered all parts of the Regent's program which promised order in the treasury and retrenchment of expenses. The generosity of the Regent and the princes of the blood who had set the example by reducing their own pensions was admirable. Nor did the Parlement wish to debate the reduction of its own privileges, particularly the right of free salt.

Then came the complaints. After a brief demur on the municipal expenses of Paris, the remonstrance came to the bills of state. The edict had given citizens several choices as to the disposal of bills of state and added that all bills not so used would cease to bear interest by the first of the year. This was unjust. On May 1, 1716, the King had guaranteed prompt payment of interest on the royal debt, and hopes had been raised that the capital could eventually be paid. Now even the interest was being destroyed. The 200 million *livres* in bills of state formed a legitimate part of the state debt. When the King converted his outstanding paper into bills of state, he had given assurance that they were secure. If the edict were registered, they would be destroyed. But beyond all this, the four methods of converting the bills of state did not suffice to use them all, and people in the provinces would not have enough time to decide which conversion was best. They would lose everything. Finally, the magistrates maintained that the poor who had invested in bills of state would lose their meager savings and face destitution.

The last part of the remonstrance dealt with the bills of the receivers-general of the finances. The edict was converting these bills from private debts of the receivers-

general into state debts. When this happened, creditors
of the receivers-general would lose their rights of collection and the state would have a new debt burden.
Creditors' rights must be sustained, for it set an example
of commercial honesty, and France did not need more
state debts. Both the treasury and the receivers-general
would be harmed by the edict. The receivers-general,
who borrowed for the account of the treasury, would have
their credit ruined and could no longer advance funds
to the King. The state would lose, for it could not get
anticipations on future tax revenue from the credit commanded by the receivers-general. The reputations of the
indivdiual receivers-general had convinced the public
to invest in their notes—that is, to buy futures in the royal
taxes. The credit of the state did not inspire such confidence. Assumption by the state of the receivers-generals'
debts would reduce royal credit still further and destroy
a source of income. The remonstrance closed with the
hope that the Regent would regard it as a reminder that
the duty of the Parlement was to represent to the King
the feelings and needs of the people.[25]

To all this the young King replied that he "received the
remonstrance of his Parlement in good part, persuaded of
its affection, obedience and zeal for the good of the
State. . . ." The Chancellor added that "His Majesty . . .
will immediately inform his Parlement of his intentions on
an edict that ought to be promptly executed, for all its
articles are only for the ease and fortunes of the peoples
of the Kingdom." [26] No one who heard this rejoinder was
in much doubt as to the Regent's views on his edict.

The remonstrance itself was a cogent document. It

[25] Text is in Flammermont (ed.), *Les Remontrances*, I, 50–53.
[26] Text is in Saint-Simon, *Mémoires*, XXXII, 107n.

gave a clearly reasoned account of why the court did not like certain provisions of the edict of August 26. Assumption by the state of the debts of the receivers-general was clearly a prelude to partial repudiation, for the state could not possibly pay. Conversion of the bills of state into other forms of government paper was also disguised repudiation. As long as there was the huge annual deficit, all the crown could ever pay was the interest, and not always that. It was quite clear that the crown would not undertake the Parlement's program of honoring at face value the entire debt. Nor would the magistrates ever accept the state debt as a speculative venture in investment. In the hard money, pre-Keynsian economic philosophy of the magistrates, payment of debts by the state was the prime path to the restoration of fiscal health. The magistrates regarded payment of debts as almost a religious obligation. They gave the Regent their advice from these assumptions.

The Regent himself wished to pay off the debt in full at par. He too thought it the correct thing to do, but he was beginning to see that he could never do so with orthodox finance. He was a man of vision—somewhat clouded vision, but vision nonetheless—and he was already attracted to the theories of John Law. Perhaps this new and dazzling financial scheme might work. But he was still undecided. He would at least save the Duke of Noailles' edict. On September 9 he sent an interpretative declaration to the court which explained and ameliorated some of the provisions of the edict which had bothered the magistrates. The crown resumed the municipal expenses of Paris. Interest was allowed after January 1, 1718, on bills of state which remained unconverted, and holders of bills of receivers-general were allowed to keep them at

4 per cent or convert them into treasury notes. The magistrates were elated. All their objections had been met. They registered the disputed articles of the edict of August 26 at once.[27] After receiving the congratulations of the First President, the magistrates adjourned for the vacations.

The Regent could not adjourn. He had to live with the problems of government, some of which he had inherited and some of which he had created. The political pretensions of the Parlement was one of the latter. On three separate occasions during the dispute the Regent had tried to save his edict, ignoring the question of his power. The edict he had worked so hard to save he himself had emasculated in the interpretative declaration of September 9. He had surrendered on everything. But all of this maneuvering had left the constitutional challenge of the refusal to register only part of an edict without comment, seemingly without notice. He had allowed the Parlement to win its point.

It was a major victory for the court. Any edict could be completely modified by simply registering some of its provisions, and royal legislation was on the way to being at the mercy of the magistrates. Moreover, having failed to meet the challenge, the Regent left in doubt his attitude toward future accumulations of power by the court. His good will overcame his good sense. A generous and genial man, the Regent hated to strike hard, and the Parlement

[27] "Registres du conseil secret de Parlement de Paris," A.N., série X (1A) 8433, fols. 422–31, September 10, 1717; "Minutes du conseil secret de Parlement de Paris," A.N., série X (1B) 8899, item 18, September 10, 1717; "Déclaration du Roy en interprétation de l'Edit du mois d'aout dernier," B.N., série F 23621 (783), September 9, 1717; Flammermont (ed.), Les Remontrances, I, 65; Dangeau, Journal, XVII, 160; Marais, Journal et Mémoires, I, 236–37.

was presented with an irresistible temptation to try to further increase its power.

The winter of 1718 looked like the right time to make that attempt. During the winter months of 1717–18, the political stock of the government stood at considerable discount. The exaggerated hope and optimism which had accompanied the new regime had worn off, and no solid achievements had been forthcoming. The promises of September, 1715, were still words. The crown was in debt, the finances were in disorder, interest on the *rentes* was in arrears. The foreign policy had about it the air of drift, and the vaunted councils had proved unworkable. While the Regent had not actually made the situation any worse, he had not been the savior he had seemed to be. It looked to Paris as if the Regent's government were merely the same old thing.

Little wonder, then, that by the middle of January rumors were circulating about the coming sessions of the Parlement. By their action in opposing increased expenditure and their willingness to give up salt privileges, the magistrates had created the impression that they were Roman senators devoted to the public weal. Many hoped that the Parlement would closely examine fiscal affairs and might even make a remonstrance on them.[28] Few thought that the Parlement ought to remain silent.

On January 14, 1718, the Parlement met to fulfill those hopes. There was no edict to discuss and register, but the magistrates had become accustomed to politics. They felt its lure and thought it right and reasonable to consider the *res publica* in general, as well as specific edicts. This was contrary to the general practice, but there were

[28] Dangeau, *Journal,* XVII, 229–30.

no objections from the Palais Royal, and the sessions proceeded.

The magistrates began with the finances. They discussed the arrears in the interest on the government bonds, or *rentes*, and the great number of offices suppressed while their holders were not reimbursed.[29] Such loss of invested capital never ceased to bother these judicial investors. The court met again on January 15 and decided to make a remonstrance on the general financial state of the realm. The First President asked the magistrates what they wished to include in their remonstrance. Angry about the fate of the bills of state and those of the receivers-general, on which interest was not being paid, the magistrates decided to ask the Regent to create a fund, in accordance with the declaration of September 9, 1717, to pay off these obligations. They would also ask the Regent to pay interest on the capital lost when offices had been suppressed out of hand. Next came the indirect taxes. The magistrates were incensed that individual exemptions to the *aides* and *gabelles* had been given to courtiers and favorites, when the edict of August, 1717, had abolished them and the magistrates had given theirs up. Only hospitals should be favored, no one else.

Then came the matter of royal officials who still had their offices. Criticizing the size of the bureaucracy, the magistrates voted to ask the Regent to eliminate duplications in offices and functions in order to save money. Pruning an entrenched bureaucracy was an eternal hope, but one which was seldom close to achievement; and

[29] *Ibid.*, XVII, 230; Saint-Simon, *Mémoires*, XXXIII, 21; Flammermont (ed.), *Les Remontrances*, I, 56; "Registres du conseil secret de Parlement de Paris," A.N., série X (1A) 8434, fol. 87, January 14, 1718; "Minutes du conseil secret de Parlement de Paris," A.N., série X (1B) 8899, item 19, January 14, 1718.

this case was no exception, for the officials owned their offices and did not wish to give them up. The First President then passed on to the unpaid interest on the *rentes*. The magistrates were great *rentiers*. They decided to order the Provost of the Merchants of Paris, Daniel Trudaine, to come before the Parlement the next day to explain the situation of the *rentes*. Like the proposed remonstrance, this was questionable procedure. While not actually forbidden, it had not been contemplated in the Declaration of Vincennes. But the personal interests of the magistrates and the public weal seemed to demand action, so the Parlement summoned Trudaine.[30]

On the morning of January 17 Trudaine made his report. He said simply that there was no money. In light of this fact, the magistrates decided to petition the Regent not to contract new debts, so that he could pay interest on his old ones. Funds for this could come from the farmers-general. Considering the absolute dependence of the crown on that consortium, there was no chance of this being adopted. The Parlement also complained that "royal funds were being diverted from the vaults of accountable officers into the hands of people having no authority to receive them." This was a clear allusion to John Law, whom the magistrates disliked, and who was beginning to have considerable influence on the Regent. The Parlement voted to ask the Regent to order "all royal funds, of whatever nature, to be put into the hands of the officers supposed to receive them . . .[and] . . . to be given to no one else on any pretext whatever. . . ." By the

[30] "Registres du conseil secret de Parlement de Paris," A.N., série X (1A) 8434, fols. 91–93, January 15, 1718; "Minutes du conseil secret de Parlement de Paris," A.N., série X (1B) 8899, item 23, January 15, 1718; Saint-Simon, *Mémoires*, XXXIII, 27; Dangeau, *Journal*, XVII, 230; Flammermont (ed.), *Les Remontrances*, I, 56–57.

end of this session, the magistrates had heard enough horror stories about the royal fisc. They decided to remonstrate.[31]

The debates of the Parlement were no secret to the Regent. Having been informed of the impending remonstrance, and knowing its probable contents, he called a Council of Regency. He told the assembled statesmen about the Parlement's activities, and asked their opinions on whether these should be allowed to continue. There was much debate over the constitutionality of the Parlement's activities, but the final consensus was that political expediency demanded that the remonstrance be heard, and the Parlement was so informed.[32]

The remonstrance was a detailed critical analysis of those elements of the fiscal confusion which affected men of substance and privilege. In September, 1717, the Parlement had pointed out the losses suffered by citizens from the funding of the bills of state, and the Regent had agreed. The Parlement also maintained that the proposed methods for disposing of the bills of state were insufficient to use them up and that those left would be worthless. Again the Regent had agreed. So there could be no disagreement with the Parlement's plan to set up a fund to pay interest on the bills of state and thus reassure the investing public.

[31] "Registres du conseil secret de Parlement de Paris," A.N., série X (1A) 8434, fols. 95–96, 103–105, January 17 and 19, 1718; "Minutes du conseil secret de Parlement de Paris," A.N., série X (1B) 8899, item 25, January 17, 1718, and item 33, January 19, 1718; Dangeau, *Journal*, XVII, 231; Saint-Simon, *Mémoires*, XXXIII, 27–28; Barthelémy (ed.), *Gazette de la Régence*, January 24, 1718, p. 220; Flammermont (ed.), *Les Remontrances*, I, 57–58.

[32] "Procès-verbal du conseil de Régence du samedi 22 janvier 1718," in Saint-Simon, *Mémoires*, XXXIII, Appendix 2, 327–28.

In September, 1717, the Regent had guaranteed 4 per cent interest to the holders of bills of the receivers-general. The receivers-general also ought to pay the capital of their bills at maturity. Having obtained royal protection freeing them from their obligations, they were paying neither the interest nor the principal. It was necessary at least to begin payment of the interest. The principal was a legitimate debt too, but there were times for leniency. Anxious for the good of the state, the Parlement asked only for convenient terms, which would give investors their money and allow the receivers-general a chance to put their affairs in order.

In August, 1717, the Parlement had registered the suppression of the free salt privileges and all other exemptions to the indirect taxes. The magistrates were convinced that the treasury would never recover if such exemptions remained. Only hospitals and charitable institutions should have privileges. Otherwise, the law applied and should be enforced, and failure to do so was prejudicial to the public good. The Parlement demanded that the edict be executed without favoritism.

After a note on the royal bureaucracy, the magistrates came to the most important point of all—the arrears in the interest on the *rentes*. Louis XIV had considered the *rentes* so important that he had engaged his royal word that they would be paid promptly. The wisest ministers believed it one of the fundamental laws of the kingdom to pay these government bonds in order to maintain credit and confidence. Loans secured by *rentes* were the easiest means of raising money in an emergency, and the most faithful subjects invested their fortunes in them. Now, however, the crown could not pay the *rentes*. Many investors had received no payment at all for 1717, which had caused consternation and a fall in government credit. The magistrates asked that payment start at once.

The remonstrance closed with a comment on John Law. One of the most important fundamental laws of France had established the Chamber of Accounts to supervise the royal funds. The Chamber of Accounts provided security for the crown and had the confidence of the people. But now royal funds were being diverted to a private bank, converted into a new kind of banknote, and no longer came under the jurisdiction of the proper authorities. The public was alarmed. The magistrates of both courts were no less so. This fiscal novelty should be discontinued, and royal funds should again be deposited with officials responsible to the Chamber of Accounts. With this relatively mild attack on John Law, the remonstrance closed.[33]

The boy King, who had sat through the entire remonstrance, replied merely that he had heard the document. Chancellor Aguesseau gave the Regent's opinions of the whole affair. He said that the "King is persuaded of the good intentions of his Parlement, and will examine in his Council what is pertinent . . . and will presently let you know his wishes."[34] The interview ended on this curt note.

When the Regent renewed the financial dialogue with his Parlement a month later, his comments were mild and calm. He clearly wished to let the remonstrance die a natural death. He did report, however, that the King had been happy to hear the remonstrance, even though

[33] Text is in Flammermont (ed.), Les Remontrances, I, 58–64.

[34] Text of the reply is in "Procès-verbal du conseil de Régence du samedi 22 janvier 1718," in Saint-Simon, Mémoires, XXXIII, Appendix 2, pp. 327–28.

it did not fall within the limits of the Declaration of Vincennes. Payment of the *rentes* would always be one of the principal objects of the crown. The King did not understand how the holders of bills of state or receivers-general had lost their investment. Nothing more; the issue was closed.[35] And the magistrates could not reopen it, for the Regent refused to discuss it further.

There can be little doubt that the Parlement greatly increased its powers and the scope of its political deliberations during the two and a half years following the session of September 2, 1715, and the Declaration of Vincennes. The magistrates had developed the habit of speaking out on vital political issues, indeed, in the case of the Gallican liberties, of almost creating those issues. The court had discussed politics without referring to a specific edict and could remonstrate at will. This was far from either the spirit or the letter of the Regent's concessions in 1715. Years of obedience had lulled the Regent and his ministers into assuming that the court's political renaissance would be tentative and halting.

This, however, had not been the case. Judicial politics in both the royal finances and the Gallican liberties were major events of the early Regency. The political climate was favorable. The trend of royal legislation concerning finances harmonized generally with the magistrates' prejudices and ideas about economics. The Parlement registered the Chamber of Justice with no difficulty and also approved the establishment of a bureau to examine, and reduce, the unfunded debt. The letters

[35] Text is in Flammermont (ed.), *Les Remontrances*, I, 65; see also Dangeau, *Journal*, XVII, 251, 259; "Registres du conseil secret de Parlement de Paris," A.N., série X (1A) 8434, fols. 189–90, March 4, 1718; "Minutes du conseil secret de Parlement de Paris," A.N., série X (1B) 8899, item 4, March 4, 1718.

patent of May, 1716, creating John Law's bank as a private institution were registered immediately. Major financial moves were well received.

But minor ones were not. This is the crux of the Parlement's successful opposition to the crown. Because the magistrates basically agreed with the Regent, the issues on which they resisted were rather easily settled, and the Parlement was able to play a role of attacking ministerial mistakes and supporting the interests of the bourgeois. A grave crisis could be handled only by the Regent. A major departure in financial matters could come only from the crown, but lesser issues could be negotiated. On these the Regent might give in, for it made little difference in the basic fiscal policy. Here the Parlement could safely make constitutional and political demands on the government. In a situation in which fundamental policies were agreed upon, the court assumed the role of protector of the people and watchdog over the misdeeds of ministers and favorites. There seemed to be no harm in allowing the Parlement to expand its role and indulge its constitutional pretensions, because even if this constitutional and political role temporarily cut deeply into the powers of the crown, policy was still saved. Such was the Regent's view. As the magistrates' Gallicanism was his own, and as their fiscal views were close to his, the Regent could allow the Parlement to expand its powers and its constitutional theories in these areas.

Basic agreement between crown and court was not, however, the condition of the Parlement's entering politics in the first place. It was quite possible for an issue to arise in which the consensus evaporated, but this did not mean that the Parlement ceased its political and constitutional activities. On the contrary, it increased the tempo and seriousness of its opposition. Employing the powers explicitly recognized by the crown, those gained in the three-year era of good feeling, and the weight of public opinion, the Parlement was to become a focus for political opposition of the most serious sort.

Such stress between the Regent and his Parlement did not exist in the three years between 1715 and the spring of 1718. Solutions to the problems which arose were found within the framework established in 1715. Yet, with the remonstrance of January, 1718, the consensus was beginning to disappear. The Regent and the Parlement were drifting into fundamental disagreement on the conduct of the royal fisc. The name John Law cropped up more and more often and produced discord each time it did. Retrenchment of expenses and the Gallican liberties were being forgotten. Instead of concentrating on areas of agreement, where the Parlement had been successful both politically and constitutionally, the court was moving into violent opposition with its prince. Slowly, inexorably, John Law would become the main issue, and then the only issue.

During the early years of his rule, the Regent had used the Parlement as an instrument of government. Medieval practice had been restored. The magistrates, like the ministers, contributed to the flow of policy. Particularly with the Gallican liberties, but also with the fisc, the Regent presented the royal will through the court to the people and the papal nuncio. Again and again he had told the nuncio that the processes of justice were sacred, and that archbishops and Jesuits must stand their trial. Courtiers and favorites were told that their pensions had to be slashed because the magistrates wished it.

But the Parlement did not think of itself as a complement to the ministry. It was part of the royal government, but an absolutely independent part. Its duty was to justice and the fundamental laws of France rather than to the man or policy of the moment. The magistrates' feeling of independence and of the sacredness of their justice far outweighed their sense of being part of the ministry and the crown councils. The Parlement, existing above temporary ministers and policies, embodied the French constitution and French justice, and its politics were eternal. Consequently, the magistrates viewed their agreement with the Regent as a pleasant accident, which might or might not continue. That it did not occasioned no surprise. The magistrates used the good feeling to widen their political scope and increase the importance of their court. The Regent might be complacent, but they were not. If the Regent were lax in enforcing the letter of the Declaration of Vincennes, the magistrates were energetic in taking advantage of this. During the months to come, in the spring and summer of 1718, the Parlement would oppose the Regent everywhere, using all the prestige and increased power of its previous successes. The magistrates had gained much by essentially cooperating with the Regent. Perhaps, strengthened, they could gain even more by opposing him.

CHAPTER V

The Coin of the Realm

THE SPRING OF 1718 was a fairly peaceful time in France. The weather was good, and the prospects for the harvest were promising. There was no hint of the plague that was to ravage the southern ports of Marseilles and Toulon. France was at peace, and the Regent's policy of an English alliance was beginning to meet with success. The quarrel over the Gallican liberties was in suspension, with neither the Pope nor the Gallican bishops sure what the next move ought to be. Although a balanced budget was still a dream, the royal finances had improved somewhat since 1715, and trade was beginning to increase after the ravages of war. The Parlement's political attempt of January had run out in the sands.

Untoward events, of course, still intruded. April, 1718, saw a tremendous fire in the heart of Paris, which started on the Pont St. Michel and burned for three days, completely out of control. A whole quarter by the river was destroyed, as well as the bridge, and the loss of life was considerable. Municipal fire protection had proved woefully inadequate. The Parlement was considering plans for rebuilding the Pont St. Michel and for improving the burned-out quarter. The magistrates had a civic as well as a national consciousness, and local as well as royal responsibilities.

The potential crisis of a minority, and a bankrupt one at that, had been passed. Cabaret songs had a gaiety they had lacked before. The world was not coming to an end, and it might even be getting better. There were no longer Jesuits and tax collectors under every bed. The Regent had provided peace and a moderate prosperity, and attention could now be turned to important things. For one, there were the scandals of the Regent's suppers. He was reputed to dine with the most debauched companions and engage in the ultimate in drunken orgies. It was rumored that the Duke of Richelieu, an affected fop, gave nude luncheons and swapped mistresses with his friends. The Regent's daughter gave lewd exhibitions for the court. Rouillé de Coudray, one of the Regent's financial advisors, was a sot, even by the Palais Royal's rather lenient standards. A young poet, Arouet de Voltaire, was in the Bastille again for maligning the Regent. Good, he deserved it. On the contrary, retorted others, he was a marvelous wit.

The Regent himself enjoyed the best of spirits. Although he drank his daily ration of six bottles of still champagne, his strong constitution seemed immune to any ill effects. While he continued his association with scandalous companions, he was no longer under suspicion of having murdered his royal relatives to become King. His outward indolence effectively masked a lively and acute intelligence. His mistresses lent his regime an air of insouciance. The Regent was beginning to find glimmers of popularity.

If the glimmers of solutions to the problems of government came so easily, the Regent would have been a happy, easy man. But, somehow, they didn't. Philippe d'Orléans had schemed and bribed to gain control over the reins of government and had succeeded. His triumph was the work of a day; the burdens of victory were the business of years. The Regent, however, was unhappy with burdens that lasted years. His was an active and lively mind, which disliked the stolid attention to detail so typical of his predecessor. The Regent had imagination; old solutions and timeworn homilies did not appeal to him. Particularly in the finances, the nagging worry of French princes, the old ways did not seem the best ways, and the Regent was perceptive enough to see that the conservative solutions were no solutions at all. If they were, then why was there a fiscal crisis in the first place? New men and new ideas, or at least the most spectacular of the old—that was what attracted the Regent. He wanted a quick, painless way out of the fiscal morass, a stupendous solution to put the problem away for ever.

The Regent's first attempt at a solution was an ancient method, but spectacular. He decided to devalue the currency. How often this had been done before, no one could count, but it had been often. The Regent's edict, registered at the *Cour des Monnaies* on May 29, 1718, called for a general recoinage of the money on the pretext of halting the depreciation of government paper. All the old specie was to be taken to the mint to be recast into the new pieces. In the process the amount of precious metal in the coins would be reduced about one third, but the face value of the coin would remain the same. Two-fifths of the money taken to the mint for recoinage by any individual could be in bills of state, which were at huge discount.[1]

[1] "Edit du Roy pour la fabrication de nouvelle espèce d'or et d'argent avec la faculté de porter à la Monnoye deux cinquintièmes en sus de billets de l'Etat," B.N., série F 23621 (930), May 29, 1718; E. J. F. Barbier, *Journal historique et anecdotique du règne de Louis XV,* ed. A. de la Villegille (Paris, 1847–56), I, 6–7; Dangeau, *Journal,* XVII, 316–17; Barthelémy (ed.), *Gazette de la Régence,* June 6, 1718, pp. 258–59; Flammermont (ed.), *Les Remontrances,* I, 68.

Currency devaluation is even now a risky and delicate business; in the Regency it was no less so. The state, always in debt, would theoretically make an enormous short-term gain by the resulting inflation. Moreover, the remainder of the unfunded debt, the bills of state, would be eliminated. Yet the crown's gain would last only as long as it received taxes in good coin and paid its bills in bad, a situation that Gresham's Law recognized as temporary. It was highly likely that the only real gain by the crown would be the silver collected at the mint and the elimination of the bills of state. But the Regent thought the attendant confusion was worth it.

On June 2 the Parlement heard about the edict and decided to investigate. Taken by surprise, the magistrates were not able to do very much right away. They could not refuse to register the edict, for it had been sent elsewhere. A radical proposal from the floor to send the *gens du Roi* to the Regent with a protest was rejected in favor of the more conservative measure of naming commissioners to look into the matter. The Parlement clearly intended to consider the recoinage.[2]

For two weeks nothing happened. People with government paper were bringing in enough coin to cover the paper and hoarding the rest. The mint was starting to issue the new money. The *Cour des Monnaies* made no protest. The Parisian public seemed uninterested, as the markets had not yet begun to show a general price rise, but the Parlement was interested. Its commissioners had not forgotten, and on June 14 the court convened to hear

[2] "Minutes du conseil secret de Parlement de Paris," A.N., série X (1B) 8899, item 4, June 2, 1718; Dangeau, *Journal*, XVII, 316; Saint-Simon, *Mémoires*, XXXV, 3.

their report. This time the radicals in the ranks could not be contained. The court voted to send deputies to discuss the edict in a joint meeting with the representatives of the other sovereign courts of Paris—the *Cour des Aides,* the *Cour des Monnaies,* and the Chamber of Accounts. A secretary was dispatched to ask the other courts to attend and to tell the *Cour des Monnaies* to bring the edict. The protest would be bolstered by seeking a written comment on the edict by six corporations of merchants and six noted bankers.

Although their sister courts were not ready to send delegates to a joint meeting on such short notice, the Parlement's deputies met that very afternoon. They called upon the representatives of the merchant guilds, who were given a single day to prepare their opinions and bring them to the court. Then came the bankers, who one after another vigorously condemned the recoinage. Having performed satisfactorily, they too were told to submit their views in writing.[3]

A joint meeting of delegates from the four sovereign courts of Paris was a major political event. Nowhere did royal legislation authorize such a meeting, and nowhere did the usual procedures of the Parlement envision one. Fundamental law, the favorite canon of the magistrates, was silent on such matters. Moreover, the event had ominous historical overtones. The last time such a meeting had occurred was during the Fronde. No prince would allow the signs of those unhappy times to reappear. Indolent though he might be, the Regent moved swiftly

[3] Barthelémy (ed.), *Gazette de la Régence,* June 17, 1718, pp. 259–60; "Registres du conseil secret de Parlement de Paris," A.N., série X (1A), 8435, fols. 370–71, June 14, 1718; "Minutes du conseil secret de Parlement de Paris," A.N., série X (1B) 8899, item 32, June 14, 1718.

now. On the fifteenth a messenger from the *Cour des Monnaies* told the Parlement that the Regent had refused them permission to attend the joint meeting. On the seventeenth the *Cour des Aides* told the same tale, and the Chamber of Accounts said that the Regent was going to decide on their request. No one had any doubt what that decision would be. The proposed joint meeting was put down.[4]

The Parlement's sessions, however, were not over. The joint meeting may have been reduced to the court's commissioners, but they went on anyway. On the afternoon of the seventeenth, the very day the Parlement learned of the collapse of the joint session, the commissioners convened to hear more from the merchants and bankers, who repeated the views the magistrates had already heard. So satisfactory were their reports that the Parlement sent the *gens du Roi* to the Regent to ask him to suspend the execution of the recoinage until the edict had been discussed and registered by the Parlement.[5]

Having crushed the incipient combination of the Parisian sovereign courts, the Regent felt reasonably certain that he could deal with the Parlement alone. He

[4] "Registres du conseil secret de Parlement de Paris," A.N., série X (1A) 8435, fols. 371–73, June 15, 1718; "Minutes du conseil secret de Parlement de Paris," A.N., série X (1B) 8899, item 33, June 15, 1718; Dangeau, *Journal*, XVII, 326–27; Barthelémy (ed.), *Gazette de la Régence*, June 20, 1718, p. 261; "Minutes du conseil secret de Parlement de Paris," A.N., série X (1B) 8899, item 34, June 17, 1718.

[5] "Registres du conseil secret de Parlement de Paris," A.N., série X (1A) 8435, fols. 372–75, June 17, 1718; "Minutes du conseil secret de Parlement de Paris," A.N., série X (1B) 8899, items 35–36, June 17, 1718; Dangeau, *Journal*, XVII, 327; Saint-Simon, *Mémoires*, XXXV, 5; E. de Barthelémy (ed.), *Les Correspondants de la Marquise de Balleroy, 1706–1725* (Paris, 1883), I, 327.

made no objection to the examination of the recoinage edict and received the *gens du Roi* in good part. Although the edict must stand, since recoinage had actually begun, the Regent would be glad to hear a remonstrance on the subject, even if the Parlement ought not to make one. He blandly remarked that the authority of the King would be upheld.[6] The magistrates did not believe him.

Having accepted the Regent's offer of a remonstrance, the magistrates appeared at the Palais Royal with their document. While the Parlement had never strayed from its proper submission to the King, whose power was ordained by God, it wished to make several reflections on an edict it knew only by the "unhappiness of all the orders of the great Kingdom." The public weal demanded their protest. The edict of recoinage should have been sent to the Parlement for registration. No other tribunal could fulfill this function. Although the *Cour des Monnaies* had been a sovereign court since 1551, the Parlement had subsequently considered many edicts on money and the finances.

The protest was a good deal stronger on the defects of the edict itself. The magistrates wished to argue the case on its merits, not engage in a precedence quarrel with a sister court. The recoinage would be a dead loss to the private citizen and would also repudiate part of the state debt, which the magistrates thought should be honored. There would be a vast, immediate rise in the prices of

[6] "Registres du conseil secret de Parlement de Paris," A.N., série X (1A) 8435, fols. 378–81, June 18, 1718; "Minutes du conseil secret de Parlement de Paris," A.N., X (1B) 8899, item 37, June 18, 1718; Balleroy, *Les Correspondants*, I, 327–28; Flammermont (ed.), *Les Remontrances*, I, 69; Dangeau, *Journal*, XVII, 328; Saint-Simon, *Mémoires*, XXXV, 5; Barthelémy (ed.), *Gazette de la Régence*, June 20, 1718, p. 262.

basic necessities. At the same time the revenue of the King would diminish by a third, because of the difference between the intrinsic and the legal value of the coinage. Commerce in general, and above all foreign commerce, would suffer a great loss because the French would pay out in good money and receive payment in bad. There would be a great increase in counterfeiting. Foreigners alone would profit, and France would be the loser. The Parlement begged the Regent to listen to the representation, give it the attention it deserved, and believe in the Parlement's attachment to the crown.

The Regent was noncommittal. The edict had not been sent to the Parlement because the *Cour des Monnaies* was competent in the field of money and finances. He would consider the inconveniences caused by the edict, but he could not withdraw it, as the new coins were already being minted and the crown had debts to pay.[7] If the magistrates were badly misjudging their prince, he had equally lost contact with them. They were angry and unhappy about the recoinage. They thought it a fraud, considered it their job to prevent fraud, and did not intend to be put off with an evasive answer. When they heard the Regent's reply, the magistrates decided to take action on their own to destroy the recoinage of the currency.

The action they took was drastic. The Parlement issued an order expressly forbidding notaries in the court's jurisdiction from making any payments or giving any receipt for payment in the new, inflated coin. Further, the court decided to make a remonstrance to obtain "Letters Patent addressed to the Court, carrying the revocation of the

[7] Text of the representation and the Regent's reply are in Flammermont (ed.), *Les Remontrances*, I, 70–74.

new edict of the monies, not registered here, as the said
edict is prejudicial to the King, the State, and the commerce and fortune of each individual. . . ." Finally, the
King would be asked for a new edict, to be registered in
the Parlement, which would regulate the coinage of
France. The order was published and distributed.[8]

This news shocked His Royal Highness. The Regent
felt that the Parlement was veering into questionable
paths. Instead of discussing the fire, the magistrates were
trying to regulate the finances. The Regent moved
quickly. The next morning the *gens du Roi* brought the
magistrates an order in council and a *lettre de cachet*. Already published, the order in council commanded acceptance of the new money and forbade the Parlement's order
to be received or obeyed. The *lettre de cachet* commanded immediate registration of the order.[9] No ameni-
ties accompanied these commands.

The magistrates were defiant. Repeated victories over
the Regent had left them relatively unimpressed with
his determination. So the Parlement refused to receive
either the order in council or the *lettre de cachet*. The
First President observed that the King made his wishes
known to the Parlement through letters patent, not orders
in council. All properly drafted commands were received

[8] *Ibid.*, I, 74; "Registres du conseil secret de Parlement de Paris,"
A.N., série X (1A) 8435, fols. 382–87, June 20, 1718; "Minutes du
conseil secret de Parlement de Paris," A.N., série X (1B), 8899, item
38, June 20, 1718; Balleroy, *Les Correspondants*, I, 328; Saint-Simon,
Mémoires, XXXV, 7; Barthelémy (ed.), *Gazette de la Régence*, June 24,
1718, p. 264.

[9] "Arrest du conseil d'Etat du Roy sur l'arrest du Parlement de
même jour," B.N., série F 23650, June 20, 1718; Buvat, *Journal de la
Régence*, I, 279; Dangeau, *Journal*, XVII, 329; Flammermont (ed.),
Les Remontrances, I, 75–76; Balleroy, *Les Correspondants*, I, 329;
Barthelémy (ed.), *Gazette de la Régence*, June 24, 1718, p. 265.

with respect, but the Parlement did not wish to consider either of these documents officially, and the *gens du Roi* could take them back.[10] Further deliberation by the Parlement produced further defiance. The session of June 21 ended with a second parlementary order. This one stated that the Parlement's previous order should be posted in the Palais de Justice and published everywhere, and that the Parlement would stay in session until the whole matter was settled.[11]

The Regent, so precipitous to reprimand the day before, was strangely indifferent to this second parlementary order. Completely reversing himself, he ignored it, saying that he was determined to uphold the royal authority, but he had said that many times before. He would hear the Parlement's remonstrance. He hoped the court would not disturb the public repose.[12] With this rather strange pronouncement the Regent began a policy of devious political meanderings, of censuring but not breaking the Parlement, of initiating a policy and letting it drift, of antagonizing his foes but not fighting them. Tension and mistrust became the motif of the Parlement's relations with its prince.

The Regent did move swiftly around the fringes of the problem. On June 22 he issued an order in council evoking from the Parlement to the person of the King all cases arising from the new edict. However, to soften the

[10] "Registres du conseil secret de Parlement de Paris," A.N., série X (1A) 8435, fols. 390–92, June 21, 1718; "Minutes du conseil secret de Parlement de Paris," A.N., série X (1B) 8899, items 39–40, June 20, 1718; Buvat, *Journal de la Régence*, I, 279; Flammermont (ed.), *Les Remontrances*, I, 76.

[11] Flammermont (ed.), *Les Remontrances*, I, 76.

[12] *Ibid.*, I, 76; Buvat, *Journal de la Régence*, I, 279; Leclercq, *Histoire de la Régence*, II, 153.

blow to the magistrates' purses, he promised de Mesmes that nothing would be done until the remonstrance had been presented. He then dismissed all the magistrates of the Parlement from the now moribund councils of the realm and cancelled their salaries. Father Pucelle, a councilor of the *Grand' Chambre,* was removed from the Council of Conscience, and Father Menguy and Ferrand, also of the *Grand' Chambre,* from the Council of the Interior.[13]

Hindsight makes statesmen of us all. Looking back to the summer of 1718, one can quite easily say what should have been done and what avoided, but it was probably more difficult at the time. For the Regent had foes other than the Parlement. The quiet of the spring was passing rapidly. France and Spain were moving swiftly toward a war which would come in 1719. Devaluation was beginning to prove unpopular, for commoners as well as princes could count, and good money was being hoarded. In the Council of Regency the Duke of Maine and his friends posed a strong opposition to the Regent which he was hard pressed to override. Included in this opposition were de Mesmes and Marshal Villeroy, a governor of the King. It was even feared by some that Villeroy might suborn part of the army against the Regent.

Accordingly the Regent took precautions. Soldiers were stationed around Paris beginning on June 17. One company was sent to Law's bank, another to the Hôtel de Ville, a third to the Bastille, and still another to the *Cour des Monnaies.* June 21 brought a reinforcement of

[13] "Arrest du conseil d'Etat du Roy sur l'arrest du Parlement de même jour," B.N., série F 23650, June 21, 1718; Buvat, *Journal de la Régence,* I, 279; Barthelémy (ed.), *Gazette de la Régence,* June 24, 1718, p. 367; Dangeau, *Journal,* XVII, 330; Flammermont (ed.), *Les Remontrances,* I, 84.

this guard; troops were stationed at the Paris markets with orders to force people to accept the depreciated currency. For over a week the troops remained in place, but there was no trouble.[14] All of Paris, from beggars to the Regent, was relieved.

No comment on these events was heard from the Parlement. The magistrates worked on their remonstrance, which was presented just as the troops were being withdrawn. The document was blunt and dealt heavily with the court's contention that it ought to register all edicts. The recoinage edict had two main faults, form and content. As to form, the edict should have been sent to the Parlement for registration instead of to the *Cour des Monnaies*, which was inadequate and contrary to precedent. Many recoinage edicts had been sent to the Parlement since 1551, and this should have been one of them. Next came the faults of the edict itself. No matter what court had considered it, it should have been rejected. Commerce would suffer an irreparable loss because of the higher prices of goods and increased wages. French goods would be priced out of the international market, causing a migration of French workers. As the intrinsic value of the silver mark was twenty-seven *livres*, and in France with the new coins it would be sixty, French merchants would pay at sixty but sell at twenty-seven, to their great loss. Beyond this all Frenchmen would lose. The holders of *rentes* or other government paper and those who had their old money recoined would lose. The edict was a tax on the whole kingdom without proper exemptions for birth or status. And it was a tax which

[14] Barthelémy (ed.), *Gazette de la Régence*, June 24, 1718, p. 266; Dangeau, *Journal*, XVII, 329; Balleroy, *Les Correspondants*, I, 328–29; Leclercq, *Histoire de la Régence*, II, 153.

would not even benefit the King. The taxes he would collect would be in devalued coin which could not be spent at its full face notation. Even the royal fisc, which was supposedly helped, would ultimately suffer.[15]

While the Regent pondered his reply to an increasingly irritated Parlement, the mint was stamping the new coins. So hurried was the job that some pieces showed the old designation under the new. But the new money was accepted. There was grumbling as well as hoarding, but the scare of the past two weeks was over, and the troops were withdrawn from the markets. Nonetheless, the whole affair had an ominous ring. Devaluation was unpopular with the people of Paris, and acceptance of the new coins could not disguise that fact. The Parlement's stand against recoinage was popular, as had been the attitude of the magistrates on the bills of state in January and their views on retrenchment of royal expenses two years previously. Paris was also Gallican and liked this in its Parlement. The popularity of the Parlement was growing, while that of the Regent was sinking rapidly. Perhaps this meant nothing, but still, as a timely publication of Cardinal Retz's memoirs of the Fronde recalled, regencies were uncertain, and the popularity of Parlements could affect affairs of state.

Even if he had wanted to, however, the Regent could hardly back down now when his new coins were in the streets. Thus, his reply to the Parlement was forceful. The King was happy to receive remonstrances when they did not attack his popularity and authority and when they had the happiness of the people for their aim. In this case, however, the King thought that the state debts ought to

[15] Text of the remonstrance is in Flammermont (ed.), *Les Remontrances*, I, 77–84.

be paid and that the devaluation would help. The King
was the source of all power in the kingdom, and all authority was his. There could be no deviation from his
orders, and the Parlement should be the first to recognize
and practice this. As for the evocation of cases arising
from the devaluation, that stood, and the King would see
justice done in a manner agreeable to all his subjects.[16]

Receipt of this news merely confirmed the magistrates
in their opinion that drastic steps were needed to halt the
currency devaluation. The Parlement voted overwhelmingly to make a third protest to the Regent, one that would
stress the magistrates' view of the registration of edicts
and the position of the court in the French constitutional
framework.[17] The new remonstrance was a long, forceful
document. It began quietly enough, stating that the
Parlement was bound "by the oath of loyalty that we have
taken to your Majesty in assuming our charges and by all
the ordinances of our Kings, which force us to examine
the edicts and other laws that are brought before us"
to see that there is nothing in them contrary to the interests of the state and the fundamental laws of the kingdom. After citing a few examples to prove that the Parlement had always examined and registered edicts, the
court proceeded to tell the Regent why this was, and
why it ought to be. The Parlement, the custodian of the
ancient and fundamental laws of the realm, was responsible for maintaining these laws. Louis XIV, the most

[16] Text is in *ibid.*, I, 85–87. See also Balleroy, *Les Correspondants*,
I, 333; Dangeau, *Journal*, XVII, 334; Saint-Simon, *Mémoires*, XXXV, 11.

[17] "Registres du conseil secret de Parlement de Paris," A.N., série X
(1A) 8435, fols. 412–16, July 4, 1718, fols. 422–23, July 8, 1718; "Minutes du conseil secret de Parlement de Paris," A.N., série X (1B) 8899,
item 6, July 4, 1718, and item 8, July 8, 1718; Dangeau, *Journal*, XVII,
334–35; Flammermont (ed.), *Les Remontrances*, I, 88.

absolute of kings, had always regarded the Parlement as the true depository of the fundamental laws of the state and had been convinced of the necessity for parlementary registration of the laws. As registration was vital for complete legality, when the Parlement did not register a bill but merely published it, the King often withdrew it. Laws sent directly to the provinces, as mentioned in the Regent's reply to the remonstrance of June 27, were of little consequence. The men who sent edicts to the Parlement knew that kings were human and could be exposed to the flattery of courtiers. The need for proper registration of laws was the same as the need for proper government of the realm. The one was a condition of the other.

The Regent himself had shown proof of his adherence to this principle as recently as 1715, when he said that he would not be satisfied with power obtained without the approval of the Parlement. As a result the magistrates had fully debated the Regent's proposals for the various councils of France, including the Council of Regency, and had awarded the powers of government to the proper person. What else could this opening session of the Regency prove but recognition of the right of the Parlement to debate affairs of state?

The magistrates then took another tack. All the preceding had been said before, without much visible result. Now the Parlement claimed to represent the voice of the people, bringing their complaints to the foot of the throne. The magistrates enlarged their own complaints into the misfortunes of France and their own remedies into the balm of an afflicted people. The remonstrance was clear and concise. "By what voice are the complaints and needs of your people able to come to your feet?" it asked. "No institution of state can be assembled without

your permission. Your Parlement, Sire, is continually assembled to render justice to your subjects in the name
and at the charge of Your Majesty; it is the only channel
by which the voice of your people can come to you, since
the Estates-General is no longer assembled." Perhaps
this claim to constitutional position and the implied threats
of popular rebuke would bring the Regent around. The
magistrates hoped so.

The final section of the document reiterated all the
evils of the edict. Trade and commerce would decay,
colonies would be lost, France would be depopulated,
usury would flourish. All the evils previously cata-
logued were repeated, and little space was wasted, for
the Regent had not responded when he had heard it before. Last came the doleful hope that the Regent might
see reason on devaluation and rescind his edict.[18]

A lengthy, vigorous document, the remonstrance presented two constitutional claims. The magistrates demanded that all edicts be registered in the Parlement no
matter what their content. No edict was law until it had
been registered by the Parlement. Further, the magistrates considered their court the legitimate voice of public opinion and its remonstrances as petitions from the nation to the King. These two claims dovetailed nicely. The
tribune of the people certainly ought to be consulted on
all laws. Registration of laws by the delegates of the
realm was not too much to ask. The Parlement asked for
a legislative veto, with no law to be published without
the consent of the court. Indeed, this view of the constitution was so ingrained with the Parlement that inclusion

---

[18] Text of the remonstrance is in Flammermont (ed.), *Les Remontrances*, I, 88–105. For a description see Balleroy, *Les Correspondants*,
I, 335–36.

of it in the remonstrance was almost casual, as if everyone understood it and ought to agree. But everyone did not agree. The Regent did not intend to surrender his legislative powers. He had to stand by his edict, for people were bringing money to the mint to be made into the new coins. Moreover, the claims advanced by the Parlement made retreat difficult, for the Regent could not afford even the appearance of giving in to the court. So he did nothing; he made no reply to the court on its remonstrance. The new coins continued to appear and the markets remained quiet. The Parlement and its protest were ignored.

In the following two weeks the political situation grew worse. The Parlement's opposition to the Regent greatly increased in scope. From 1715 until August, 1718, the Parlement contented itself with remonstrances and the suppression of ultramontane literature. On occasion, in August, 1717, and again in January, 1718, the Parlement had tried to modify the fiscal policies of the crown. But these attempts had been short-lived, and nothing had come of them. A single refusal by the Regent had sufficed to put them down. Disagreements had not passed beyond written protests. Bits and pieces of royal policy were challenged, but major elements were not, and the Parlement had not enunciated a policy of its own. This, however, began to change in June, 1718, with the parlementary order telling the people not to accept the new money. On August 1 the magistrates began to enlarge on this. From the August sessions there emerged a parlementary fiscal policy at variance with the views of the Regent and his advisors. The caste and professional prejudices of the magistrates came to the surface. The shibboleths of the wealthy, the conservatism of legists, half-formed notions of mercantilism—all were contained in the actions taken by the Parlement.

The most immediate concern was fiscal responsibility, in this case payment of interest on the various forms of government paper. The magistrates were great *rentiers*, holding vast sums of government bonds as a major outlet for their liquid wealth. Interest on this investment had been sporadic since the Spanish Succession and had not improved much during the Regency. Numerous complaints had been made before 1718, and they were redoubled now. The magistrates, and the *rentiers* they represented on this issue, did not want their interest to be paid in the new, devalued coin any more than they had previously wanted payment in paper. For the wealthy bourgeois, and for many nobles as well, prompt payment of interest on government paper was the test of fiscal health.

By this standard the royal fisc was gravely ill, and confidence, so necessary to the lending class, had all but disappeared. As all other conventional standards seemed to point in the same direction, the Parlement had no hesitation about embarking on this adventure of establishing its own fiscal policy. Beginning on August 1 the court met to discuss royal financial policy in its entirety and to propose any changes which might appear necessary to improve the regularity of interest payments.[19] The *rentes* and other government paper were the main topics of discussion. On August 9 Trudaine, the Provost of the Merchants of Paris, was called to the Palais de Justice

[19] "Registres du conseil secret de Parlement de Paris," A.N., série X (1A) 8435, fols. 492–93, August 1, 1718; "Minutes du conseil secret de Parlement de Paris," A.N., série X (1B) 8900, item 1, August 1, 1718; Flammermont (ed.), *Les Remontrances*, I, 105.

to give an account of the *rentes* constituted on the income of the Hôtel de Ville.[20] When asked for a complete accounting of the various issues of *rentes*, Trudaine replied that a statement had been begun several days previously, but that there were many difficulties. Over 70 types and issues of *rentes* were current, and there had been over 150 others, not all of which had been completely funded. In spite of this, progress was being made, and Trudaine hoped eventually to have a complete statement on the *rentes*. The provost was ordered to return on August 17, and again on December 1, to give further reports.[21]

The financial situation appeared so serious to the magistrates that they decided to go beyond merely questioning the Provost of the Merchants. If the Regent was not going to take proper care to guard the interest on government obligations, the Parlement would have to. By an overwhelming majority the magistrates voted to inaugurate their own fiscal policy. An order was passed stating that if the King were obliged to issue new *rentes* on the revenues of Paris, the Provost of the Merchants and the syndics of the city could sign the contract only up to the sums mentioned in the edict.[22] This was a considerable reform. Although the declarations establishing *rentes* on the income of Paris always mentioned the terms and the number of shares to be sold, the crown was in the habit of selling as many *rentes* as people would buy, regardless of whether the income covered them. Such stock

---

[20] Flammermont (ed.), *Les Remontrances,* I, 105.

[21] "Registres du conseil secret de Parlement de Paris," A.N., série X (1A) 8435, fols. 522–25, August 9, 1718; "Minutes du conseil secret de Parlement de Paris," A.N., série X (1B) 8900, item 30, August 9, 1718.

[22] "Registres du conseil secret de Parlement de Paris," A.N., série X (1A) 8435, fols. 526–27, August 11, 1718; Flammermont (ed.), *Les Remontrances,* I, 105–106.

watering had become an important part of the government loans. The Parlement's proposal to end it would
cut into the royal revenue, something the Regent could
hardly allow. It would interfere with the royal prerogative concerning the finances, something else the Regent
could not permit. This attempt at regulation of the
royal finances could only be resisted, and the differences
between court and prince grew.

On August 12 the magistrates returned to the attack.
They began to consider John Law and his growing influence on the fiscal policies of the realm. The magistrates'
objections to Law were numerous. They did not like
his financial theories. While most of the magistrates had
no real idea what Law's economic views were, he was
obviously not a traditional mercantilist. He did not appear to believe in retrenchment of royal expenses, the
hallowed tax exemptions of the nobility, or even the old
taxes themselves. He was a man of novelties, and the
magistrates were men of tradition. John Law's bank was
becoming an important cog in the royal fiscal system.
His notes were currency. Tax receipts were deposited
with Law; royal debts and obligations were being discharged by Law's bank and with Law's notes. The magistrates felt that this was all outrageous, in complete defiance of the old methods and the old laws. Royal funds
ought to be deposited with officers accountable to the
Chamber of Accounts, and royal obligations should be
discharged by responsible officials. Such men had pledged
their entire fortunes to cover any losses the fisc might
suffer, and their personal honor was bound up with that
of the King. Was Law so bonded? Was his honor so
committed?

After a long discussion of Law's bank and the rights of

foreigners to bank in France, the indignant magistrates passed an order. It began by stating that the Parlement

commands that the ordinances and the edicts creating officers of finances, and the Letters Patent of 2 and 20 May, 1716, establishing the said bank . . . will be executed according to their form and tenor, that the bank will remain reduced to the terms and the operations carried in the said Letters Patent, and in consequence, forbids the director . . . and all other employees of the said bank to guard or hold . . . any royal funds in the vaults . . . nor make any use or employment of royal funds for the account of the bank nor to the profit of those who run it under the punishments fixed by ordinance. . . . Royal funds [are] to be remitted to the accountable officers in order to be used by them in the exercise of their functions, and . . . all the said officers [are] to be responsible in their own names, each in his own account, of all the funds of their management. . . . Further, the said Court forbids all foreigners, even naturalized, from involving themselves, directly or indirectly, under their own names or an intermediary, in the management and administration of the royal funds. . . .[23]

The Regent found this sort of thing completely unacceptable. Remonstrances, perhaps, they were only protests and could be ignored. But these parlementary orders were a demand that France cease doing as the Regent wished and start doing as the Parlement wished. Had the Declaration of Vincennes given the Parlement the right to govern? As long as the magistrates had confined themselves to remonstrances or the sup-

[23] "Registres du conseil secret de Parlement de Paris," A.N., série X (1A) 8435, fols. 530–33, August 12, 1718; "Minutes du conseil secret de Parlement de Paris," A.N., série X (1B) 8900, item 31, August 12, 1718. Text is in Flammermont (ed.), *Les Remontrances*, I, 106–107; "Arrest de la Cour de Parlement," B.N., série F 23672, August, 1718; Barbier, *Journal historique et anecdotique*, I, 7–8.

pression of ultramontane literature, the Regent was willing to make concessions and even use the court as an instrument of government policy. But such indulgence
vanished when the court gave evidence of wishing to
govern. On August 21 the Regent, therefore, sent the
Parlement an order in council to be registered. It dras-
tically limited the political powers of the Parlement and
returned the court to the position which the Regent
thought it ought to have.

No pleasantries were wasted. The opening sentence
declared that the Parlement, led astray by bad council,
had "abused the different marks of confidence His Majesty
has had the honor to give it. . . ." The court had continuously tried to diminish the royal authority and take
over the management of finances. It held itself superior
to the other sovereign courts, particularly the *Cour des
Monnaies*. It had made a remonstrance after the time
alloted for one in the Declaration of Vincennes. It had
forbidden a royal order in council to be obeyed and almost given up the administration of justice for politics.
The Parlement had reduced confidence in the government
and meddled in affairs where it had no competence.

Because of these sins the Regent ordered a number of
reforms in the parlementary procedures. The Parlement
could continue to make remonstrances, but they must
be made within a week of the receipt of the edict in question and according to the form prescribed in the Declaration of Vincennes. It was forbidden, however, to make
any remonstrance on an edict not sent for registration, as
with the edict on recoinage. If the Parlement failed to
remonstrate within a week, the edict would be considered
registered, would be published, and if the court contra-
vened such an edict, the King would annul the action of

the Parlement. The King would inform the *gens du Roi* whether he would receive a remonstrance. If he heard it and still wished the edict to be registered, that would be done at once, or the edict would be published anyway. Only then could the court make a second remonstrance. The Parlement could not under any circumstances modify a royal edict, and it was forbidden to invite the other sovereign courts to a common meeting without the written consent of the King. The Parlement was further forbidden to deliberate on the finances or take any cognizance of the affairs of state unless the King asked for advice. In the tenth and last article of his order in council the King annulled all parlementary orders against the devaluation of the coinage. Parlementary proclamations against John Law were also annulled. Finally, the King wished this order in council registered and published by the Parlement.[24]

The Parlement ignored the order in council. After three years of concessions from the Regent, it was hard to tell when he meant business. On August 22 the court met and debated politics and finances, sending the *gens du Roi* to the Regent to ask what had become of the bills of state received from the Chamber of Justice and the Mississippi lottery. Had they been burned? The magistrates wished to know. The *gens du Roi* were instructed to return on August 26 and tell the magistrates the results of their mission.[25] The Regent and his advisers were

[24] Text is in Isambert and others (eds.), *Recueil général,* XXXI, 159–62; "Minutes du conseil secret de Parlement de Paris," A.N., série X (1B) 8900, item 61, August 21, 1718.

[25] "Registres du conseil secret de Parlement de Paris," A.N., série X (1A) 8435, fol. 589, August 22, 1718; "Minutes du conseil secret de Parlement de Paris," A.N., série X (1B) 8900, item 62, August 22, 1718.

shocked by this disregard for the royal will. The same day the *gens du Roi* appeared the Regent began plans for a *lit de justice*. If the Parlement would not listen to reason, he would smash it. He would restore things to their proper order, with the prince, not the court, as the master.

In recounting these events it is all too easy to fall into the practice of assuming that the Parlement greatly exceeded its constitutional authority and position and ought to have been quashed, or that the Regent greatly exceeded his and was acting the part of a tyrant. Yet it is not that simple. There was plenty of room in Old Regime France for legitimate disagreement on how the state should be governed. Almost every conceivable aspect of a constitutional issue could be buttressed with hoary precedents and distinguished legal arguments. The French monarchy was old, and there was a precedent for nearly everything. Both the crown and the Parlement had, at some time, argued both sides of nearly every issue. This was not simply the result of the absence of a written constitution. We are all aware that the mere possession of such a document does not end constitutional debate; quite the reverse is true. What seems clear was that the Regent and the magistrates honestly differed considerably on the proper method of governing the nation, and each was prepared to back his views as far as possible.

The roots of the problem lay in the enormous gap between the reality of how France was governed in the Old Regime and the constitutional self-conceptions both sides had of how it ought to be governed. In fact, the organs of government were constantly evolving, never stable or fixed. Change, while not nearly so rapid as today, was still a factor of the French monarchy. Offices, titles, functions—all underwent continuous amendment. Perhaps one example will suffice to illustrate for all. The King had once been represented in the provinces by the *prévôt*. The title and office still existed in the eighteenth century, and at least one *prévôté* court, the Châtelet in Paris, retained considerable importance, Philip Augustus replaced the *prévôt* with the *bailli* and his *baillage*. Richelieu relied on governors of provinces and intendants. Louis XIV ignored the governors and brought the powers of the intendants up as far as the crown could manage. Yet all these offices still remained, were filled, and had functions. They had simply changed. In replacing traditional fiscal institutions with John Law's bank, the Regent was following an old custom.

This change had all been in the direction of centralizing political power and authority in the hands of the King and reducing the privileges and immunities of the nobles, towns, and provinces. By the time of Louis XIV the King had acquired a strong, centralized, bureaucratic monarchy. This royal centralization provoked two rather different reactions—absolutism and a fierce resistance to further loss of local privilege. The Parlement increasingly supported the latter position, particularly as the powers of the crown began to encroach on the traditional prerogatives of the court. The magistrates began to talk about fundamental laws of the realm and the necessity for the King to respect the established way of doing things. This blanket conservatism upheld the Gallican liberties and condemned John Law.

The Regent was only marginally concerned with the theories of royal absolutism. He was oriented toward problems, not principles. He did not often ask what the legal precedents and theories were for an edict he wished to write. Instead he usually asked of his ministers: what is to be done? If a project seemed good, he went ahead, regardless of custom and particular laws, firmly believing he had the right to dispense with both. John Law's innovations seemed likely to produce good, and the prince was determined to see them through.

The magistrates, while always theoretically conceding the royal right to change custom and individual laws at pleasure, found it difficult to so in specific cases. They were always stumbling over a fundamental law or two, as opposed to simple custom. Thus John Law could do anything he wanted as long as the nobility remained undisturbed in their privileges and exemptions and the prerogatives of the sovereign courts were undiminished. But these privileges, exemptions, and prerogatives were so numerous that anything the Regent did was bound to affect one of them. The difficulty in establishing a firm line between custom and fundamental law was considerable, and the magistrates did not hesitate to draw it on the conservative side of an issue. As the fundamental laws were the immutable constitution of France, any issue could easily become a parlementary crisis.

Thus a disagreement over taxation evolved into a constitutional issue, with both sides invoking the immutable and divine constitution of France. By easy stages each side had become convinced of the other's bad faith. The Regent was a tyrant. The Parlement was filled with anarchists. Such were the judgments of the contemporaries. They belong to the eighteenth century. All we can do now is record and explain them.

CHAPTER VI

Lit de Justice

POLITICAL RUMORS of all sorts eddied through the capital during most of August. As early as August 21 men whispered knowingly about a possible *lit de justice*.[1] Nothing was certain, and there were no clearly recognizable signs that such a ceremony was imminent. No preparations had been seen at the Palais de Justice, nor had warnings been given to the magistrates. But on August 18 John Law had moved into the Palais Royal, alleging that the Parlement had planned to kidnap and hang him. Moreover, it was obvious that the Parlement had no intention of obeying the declaration of August 21. It was going to continue investigating the fiscal condition of the crown. The magistrates were simply ignoring the Regent's orders. Something had to be done, so there were rumors that something would be done.

Until this latest episode with the money and the fiscal inquisition, the Regent had not taken the politics of the Parlement very seriously. Other matters occupied his attention, and, in any case, the Parlement could not really hurt him. The Regent was greatly concerned with foreign policy and had made considerable efforts to join Great Britain in an alliance to guarantee both thrones and keep the peace in Europe.[2] Finances were equally im-

---

[1] Dangeau, *Journal*, XVII, 362.

[2] Saint-Simon, *Mémoires*, XXXV, 30–31. See the monumental work of Alfred Baudrillart, *Philippe V et la Cour de France* (Paris, 1890–1901).

portant. Regular methods had not brought order to the royal fisc, and now John Law promised a financial miracle. In addition, the Regent still faced serious enemies within his own council from the partisans of the Duke of Maine. Such major considerations took precedence over a fractious Parlement.

The politics of the Parlement had not been entirely distasteful to the Regent. The Gallicanism of the magistrates had been extremely convenient, allowing the Regent to attack the Jesuits and embarrass the Pope at one remove. The fiscal opposition of the Parlement had not hindered the crown in any serious way. Even the two remonstrances on recoinage were merely irritating. The new money was accepted in the markets, and, as a method of reducing outstanding government paper, the scheme was a success. There had not even been a street riot.

But the magistrates showed no signs of limiting themselves to remonstrances on coins; they preened themselves with dangerous constitutional doctrines. They called themselves the voice of the people and said they were tribunes, who guarded men against despotism. They claimed to be the guardians of the fundamental laws of France, which upheld the rights of all against the tyranny of the crown. A share in the formation of financial policy was the least of the magistrates' demands. The Regent had been gracious until now, but he could hardly make further allowances. Soft words had not turned away any blows. Some day, on some issue, the Parlement might raise a public outcry sufficient to force a change in policy, and it was the Regent's duty to forestall that.

He began secretly to prepare a *lit de justice,* making plans with his one trusted friend, the Duke of Saint-Simon. Perhaps Saint-Simon lacked tact and political

acumen, but he was a close friend. A man of independence and honor, the peppery little duke had stayed by
the Duke of Orléans during the hard years under Louis
XIV when all others had fled. The Regent never forgot
his loyalty, although he found Saint-Simon politically in-
competent. In this instance, however, when the need for
loyalty outweighed all other considerations, the Regent
turned to him.

The *lit de justice* was planned for the Tuileries, to pre-
serve secrecy and to prevent any possible counteraction
on the part of the Parlement. Saint-Simon himself went
to Fontanieu, chief of the furnishings of the Tuileries,
and showed him how a *lit de justice* was set up, where
everyone sat, and what furnishings were needed. He
urged Fontanieu to begin work at once and swore him
to secrecy.[3] The Regent and Saint-Simon left nothing to

[3] Saint-Simon, *Mémoires*, XXXV, 24–236. In this famous passage,
the Duke of Saint-Simon gives a long and very detailed description of
the events leading up to the *lit de justice*. He was one of the very
few in on the secret and was obviously proud of the fact. His own part
in the drama was both efficient and honorable and loses nothing in his
telling of it. Numerous details of the secret preparations to strike at
the Parlement and the Duke of Maine are given, and Saint-Simon's
fear that the Regent would get cold feet and back out comes through
clearly. Finally, the duke describes the decisive Council of Regency
which immediately preceded the ceremony.

In a history of the Parlement it would be superfluous to recount
these preparations in the detail in which Saint-Simon describes them.
Only the necessary outline will be given, along with such material as
pertained to the Parlement. This is certainly one of the most accurate
parts of the duke's memoirs. Nearly every detail can be verified from
other sources, and the mood it evokes has about it the ring of truth. In
this instance, I have relied heavily on Saint-Simon.

Finally, this section of the huge memoir is a major literary triumph.
The entire description is alive with fire and vigor, for the duke really
cared about the outcome of this day's work. His hatred for the magistrates and the royal bastards gives the whole section a hard, glittering

chance. Officers and soldiers of known loyalty were put
on the alert and provided with powder and shot. The
commander of the French Guards was ordered to be ready
on the morning of August 26 should the Parlement refuse
to come to the Tuileries. Not until four o'clock on the
morning of August 26 were the peers and marshals sent
letters instructing them to appear at the approaching *lit
de justice*.[4] The experience gained in 1715 was put to
good use.

On the morning of August 26 the decisive Council of
Regency met. Here the Regent explained for the first
time the program of the ceremony. The order in council
of August 21 which limited the powers of the Parlement
was going to be registered. The illegitimate princes were
going to be crushed once and for all by having their rank
as prince of the blood revoked and losing their places in
the line of succession to the throne. To make the disgrace of the Duke of Maine even clearer, an edict would
be registered restoring the rank and rights of his discreet
and gentle brother the Count of Toulouse.

None of the councilors was surprised at the action taken
to restrict the powers of the Parlement. But the location
and the immediacy of the *lit de justice*, and the secrecy
of its preparation, caused uneasy murmurs. And the action against the Duke of Maine shocked all but the conspirators. The Regent supported it, saying that it was only
just to the peerage that the illegitimate princes be reduced to their rightful rank of peer. The Regent also sup-

---

tone of satisfied revenge. Excitement, anticipation, and triumph are
etched here for all to read. See also the photograph of the diagram
and the explanation of a *lit de justice* in Saint-Simon's hand in *ibid.*,
XXXV, between pages 328 and 329.

[4] *Ibid.*, XXXV, 160; Barbier, *Journal historique et anecdotique*, I,
9–10.

ported restoring the rank of prince to the Count of Toulouse as a reward for his loyal conduct. The Council approved both edicts, though the several friends of the Duke of Maine were silent and unhappy. The coup was halfway home.[5]

The Parlement had opened its session at six o'clock on the morning of August 26 expecting to hear the preliminary report of the Provost of the Merchants on the *rentes*. Instead, they received the royal herald, who informed the magistrates that they must come to the Tuileries for a *lit de justice*. After much uneasy hesitation, the magistrates set out to meet their King. They walked two abreast through the town wearing their ceremonial red robes trimmed with fur. A large crowd watched, more from curiosity than support. At the Tuileries they passed under the windows of the royal council chamber, and the members of the Council of Regency hung out of the windows like little boys to watch the procession pass.[6]

The atmosphere for this ceremony was far different from that of September, 1715. The Duke of Orléans was now Regent, not a suppliant for the powers of office. The magistrates were not being asked to decide the fate of the realm. Now the peers were confident and assured, and none more so than the proud Saint-Simon, reveling

[5] Saint-Simon, *Mémoires*, XXXV, 180–215, gives all the details concerning the meeting of the Council of Regency. See also Villars, *Mémoires*, IV, 113–14; Barthelémy (ed.), *Gazette de la Régence*, August 29, 1718, p. 277. See Isambert and others (eds.), *Recueil général*, XXI, 163–66, for the texts of the edicts concerning the Duke of Maine and the Count of Toulouse.

[6] "Minutes du conseil secret de Parlement de Paris," A.N., série X (1B) 8900, item 66, August 26, 1718; Flammermont (ed.), *Les Remontrances*, I, 107; Barbier, *Journal historique et anecdotique*, I, 9; Saint-Simon, *Mémoires*, XXXV, 161; Barthelémy (ed.), *Gazette de la Régence*, August 29, 1718, p. 276.

in his revenge. He sat in his place on the high bench, and looked out "on all the Parlement, seeing astonishment, silence, consternation . . . the first president humbled, the other presidents disconcerted, attentive to all, furnishing an agreeable spectacle. . . ." [7]

All eyes turned toward Argenson. "The Keeper of the Seals remained a few moments in his chair, immobile, looking down, and the fire of his anger seemed to constrict the heart. An extreme silence eloquently announced the fear, attention, uneasiness, curiosity, of the various spectators. . . ." [8] Often, as lieutenant-general of the police

[7] Saint-Simon, *Mémoires*, XXXV, 221. There are three manuscript copies of the minutes of the *lit de justice* of August 26, 1718, and numerous contemporary publications of the proceedings of this famous and dramatic event. One of the manuscripts, copied on parchment by a secretary of the court, is part of the registers of the Parlement: "Registres du conseil secret de Parlement de Paris," A.N., série X (1A) 8435, fols. 595–626, August 26, 1718. The other copies, on rag paper and with many corrections, are in the minutes of the Parlement. One, signed by First President de Mesmes and copied verbatim into the registers, was the first draft of the official version: "Minutes du conseil secret de Parlement de Paris," A.N., série X (1B) 8900, item 68, August 26, 1718. This is the version which Flammermont used, and all notes in this chapter refer to it. See Flammermont (ed.), *Les Remontrances*, I, 170–71.

Still a third manuscript exists. This version of the *lit de justice* is: "Minutes du conseil secret de Parlement de Paris," A.N., série X (1B) 8900, item 70, August 26, 1718. It was not signed by de Mesmes. It contains numerous corrections in the hand of Argenson and bears his signature. The Keeper of the Seals obviously did not trust the magistrates to put the entire humiliation of the session into their registers and edited the first draft himself to see that they did. No slur against the Parlement is omitted or glossed over. It is from this version that de Mesmes was permitted to make his copy, which was verified and which he signed. The second draft, that signed by de Mesmes, was then copied into the registers, as was the usual procedure. Thus we have an extraordinarily reliable source, verified by both the crown and the court.

[8] Saint-Simon, *Mémoires*, XXXV, 223.

of Paris, Argenson had run afoul of the Parlement. Only a year before a president of the Parlement had boasted that he would hang him, but now the able and brutal Argenson was the master. The Keeper of the Seals turned at once to the main matter of the day, the duties and obligations of the Parlement.

. . . the King holds today his *lit de justice* for a most important affair, which concerns his glory and the repose of his people; it is the question of assuring his authority. The King cannot see without some pain that his Parlement wishes to usurp his royal authority, and that Company, not content to make its remonstrances before registering his ordinances and his edicts, has abrogated to itself the right of acting and ordering against the precise and literal disposition of his royal will.

It even seems that it has carried its enterprise to the point of pretending that the King can do nothing without the advice of his Parlement, and that his Parlement has no need of either the order or the consent of His Majesty to do what it pleases.

It is proof of such principles that the Company has rendered several orders, namely those of June 20, and the 12th of this month, and ordered the same day that these be read, published, and sent to the bailiffs and senechals . . . while many edicts of His Majesty have remained more than a year without registration and consequently without execution. Thus the Parlement can do all without the King, and the King can do nothing without the Parlement, which would soon become the necessary legislator of the Kingdom, and it would only be through its good pleasure that the King would be able to let his subjects know what his intentions were. Can the King fail to reclaim and conserve rights as sacred as these?

His Majesty would have preferred not to include in the same law judicious magistrates who have resisted with wise and constant advice the spirit of criticism, obstinacy, and presumption that has made the others act, but the law is general, and it is not possible to distinguish those of his Parlement whose prudence and fidelity merit praise, from those whose speech and actions are equally reprehensible.[9]

The reading of the order of August 21 and the homily on duty made a striking and profound impression on the magistrates. Argenson had spoken slowly, so nothing was missed, and his forceful manner of speaking impressed the magistrates as much as the words themselves. From their enemy Argenson there would be no mercy. No one took more delight in these solemn proceedings than Saint-Simon, who observed "that those magistrates so proud, for whom haughty remonstrances had not as yet satisfied pride and ambition, were struck by a chastisement so strong and so public, which turned the ignominious truth back upon them. . . ."[10] He and his fellow peers relished the suffering and desolation of the "proud bourgeois" over the complete and humiliating loss of their political power.

Although they could hardly hope to change the outcome of the ceremony, the magistrates went through the forms of protest and voting. The advocate-general Lamoignon maintained that the court had never departed from its due respect to the King. It had always been faithful and performed its duty. The order of August 21 gravely affected the Parlement and ought to be considered at great length. Lamoignon asked the King to reflect on it and on the speech he had allowed Argenson to make. If the King persisted, which could hardly be doubted, then the magistrates would proceed to registration. Lamoignon was followed by de Mesmes, who echoed the court's wish

[9] Flammermont (ed.), Les Remontrances, I, 109-10.
[10] Saint-Simon, Mémoires, XXXV, 226.

to deliberate on the order. The Keeper of the Seals merely retorted: "The King wishes to be obeyed at once."[11]

Following the reduction of his political enemy, the Regent turned to a personal one. Reading his second speech, Argenson maintained that the "King, having judged it necessary to render to the dukes and peers the rank and prerogatives which they have ceased to enjoy, also believes it necessary for the comte de Toulouse to retain all the honors he has. . . ."[12] He then read one edict reducing the illegitimate princes of the blood and a second restoring the rank of the Count of Toulouse.

This was perhaps the high point of Saint-Simon's life. He had triumphed completely. The natural princes and the despised Parlement had been humiliated before his very eyes and with his active assistance. Two of his greatest ambitions had been realized. After reading the two edicts, Argenson asked for the opinion of the Parlement, starting with the princes and the peers. Here Saint-Simon capped his triumph by saying the right thing for once. He told the Keeper of the Seals that the peers could not give an opinion on a matter in which they were an interested party. A murmur of approval followed this moderate and generous stand. The magistrates of the Parlement, however, knew what was expected of them and voted in favor of registration.[13]

The magistrates' trials were not yet finished. Argenson then announced that the King wanted the various edicts, orders, and letters patent presented during the *lit de justice* to be drawn up immediately. He did not trust

[11] *Ibid.*, XXXV, 226–27; Flammermont (ed.), *Les Remontrances*, I, 110–12; Saint-Simon called this speech of de Mesmes ". . . full of malice . . . and insolence for the regent and insolence for the king."

[12] Flammermont (ed.), *Les Remontrances*, I, 112.

[13] Saint-Simon, *Mémoires*, XXXV, 232.

the Parlement. Unaccountable delays might occur. Thus he brought the necessary papers from his own desk to the secretary of the Parlement and dictated the formulas to be used in publishing the edicts. They were signed in the King's presence. The silent magistrates sat through it all, observers at their own downfall.

In spite of the outward show of triumph provided by the *lit de justice,* neither the Regent nor his advisors thought that this would permanently eliminate the Parlement's political ambitions. The magistrates had seemed submissive enough on August 26, but how would they feel about the ceremony the next day? It might be well to ensure continued submission. So the Regent, although capable of extraordinary political apathy, resolved this time on a major show of strength. His order in council of August 21 had not really cut into the Parlement's powers, merely regulated their use. No institutional gain made during the Regency had been revoked. The *lit de justice,* humiliating though it was, had been used only to register the order in council. Something more was needed. The troops could not be called out for nothing. Urged on by Argenson, who distrusted the Parlement and personally disliked several of its presidents, the Regent resolved to show the magistrates that the *lit de justice* should not be considered an isolated event, but the pattern of the future. On the night of August 28, three councilors of the Parlement were arrested and exiled from Paris. Nine musketeers, led by officers, appeared at the door of each magistrate's house, presented him with a *lettre de cachet,* and led him off. President Blamont of the second Chamber of Inquests was sent to the Iles d'Hyères; Armand de Saint-Martin, also of the second

Inquests, to Belle-Isle; and Denis-Joseph Feydeau, of the fourth Inquests, was exiled to the Ile d'Oléron.[14]

The next morning the Parlement convened at five o'clock to deal with the backlog of judicial work left undone during the political crisis. This was almost immediately interrupted by the news of the arrests. As soon as he heard, the First President called the whole court together and told them the news. De Mesmes also called the *gens du Roi,* who were with the Regent, to hear their advice and any word from the throne. Since the *gens du Roi* could add nothing, the magistrates decided to make a remonstrance. Application to the Regent for clemency might bring results, but further resistance would not. For his part the Regent agreed to hear a remonstrance that very afternoon.[15]

De Mesmes led the delegation to the Tuileries to deliver the short, hasty document. After the *lit de justice* the magistrates had not believed that anything could increase their consternation and despair, but the news of the arrest and exile of the three magistrates had. If the King believed them guilty of some crime, he should allow the Parlement to examine them, and justice would be done. If found guilty, they would be punished as severely as possible. It would be a calamity if the liberty

[14] René Louis Voyer, Marquis d'Argenson, *Journal et Mémoires,* ed. E. J. B. Rathéry (Paris, 1859–67), I, 23; Dangeau, *Journal,* XVII, 373; Flammermont (ed.), *Les Remontrances,* I, 116; Balleroy, *Les Correspondants,* I, 346–48; Barbier, *Journal historique et anecdotique,* I, 16; Buvat, *Journal de la Régence,* I, 330; Saint-Simon, *Mémoires,* XXXV, 267–68; Barthelémy (ed.), *Gazette de la Régence,* September 2, 1718, p. 281.

[15] *Gazette de France,* September 3, 1718; "Registres du conseil secret de Parlement de Paris," A.N., série X (1A) 8435, fols. 625–29, August 29, 1718, "Minutes du conseil secret de Parlement de Paris," A.N., série X (1B) 8900, item 75, August 29, 1718.

of deliberating according to their consciences were denied
the magistrates, for then the truth could never come to
the throne. The Parlement hoped to appease the anger
of the King, but if that were not possible, it awaited new
blows, "more serious, if that can be, than the first. . . ."
The remonstrance ended with a reminder to the King that
the Parlement was a department of state and again asked
for the release of the exiled magistrates.[16]

Argenson made a short reply. The affairs of the King
required secrecy, and the conduct of the Parlement alone
would determine the King's attitude.[17] Returning to the
Palais de Justice, the magistrates discussed the events of
the day. They sent the *gens du Roi* to the Regent and
decided to suspend their judicial functions until the
prisoners were released.[18]

Reconvening on August 31, the magistrates immediately
called on the *gens du Roi*. Lamoignon de Blancmesnil reported that they had spoken to the Regent every day
since the arrest, but with no results. Each request for
release had been met with the observation that the matter
was an affair of state and must be kept secret. The Regent
repeated that his attitude depended on the Parlement's
behavior. Having heard this, Lamoignon felt that he
ought to advise the magistrates on their suspension of
justice. It could hardly please the Regent. Many families
and cases suffered from the judicial holiday, which had
lasted over two weeks already. The public good demanded that justice be recommenced. It would do no
good to press for the release of the magistrates if the

[16] Text is in Flammermont (ed.), *Les Remontrances*, I, 116–17.
[17] *Ibid.*, I, 117–18.
[18] "Registres du conseil secret de Parlement de Paris," A.N., série X
(1A) 8435, fols. 630–31, August 29, 1718.

Parlement continued to defy the crown. The Parlement could only agree, and decided to reopen the judicial sessions and continue to petition for the freedom of the exiles.

The lines of conduct were set. The Parlement would resume its ordinary functions, and the Regent, after a sufficient amount of time, would free the three judges. The eventual outcome was never in doubt. Repression and suspicion too long maintained become persecution, and the Regent wished to avoid this. Government was easier to conduct with the friendship of the Parlement, a view he relayed to the court on September 3 and again on September 5.[19] He merely wished to convince the magistrates that their politics had limits, that their conduct was scrutinized, that their company had its place. He had no intention of crushing the court, for it enjoyed considerable popular support and added to the stability of the crown. He wished only to restore it to its proper position in relation to himself.

The magistrates did not see the problem in quite the same way. They were as concerned about their exiled colleagues as was the Regent, but for far different reasons. For the Regent they were a problem of state; for the Parlement they were hostages to fortune and the crown. Differences in constitutional philosophies might be forgotten for a while in an effort to obtain the release of the exiled members, but the Parlement did not intend to be put in the shade permanently. Nor could the magistrates accept the Regent's view of their proper relationship to the crown. In the interim, however, this could

---

[19] "Registres du conseil secret de Parlement de Paris," A.N., série X (1A) 8435, fol. 654, September 5, 1718; "Minutes du conseil secret secret de Parlement de Paris," A.N., série X (1B) 8900, item 9, September 3, 1718.

be put aside. When the Parlement met on the fifth, it again considered the methods most likely to gain results. Lamoignon reported that the Regent was satisfied with the conduct of the court but could not yet act. The Regent's attitude had changed, however, and the three might be liberated soon. The *gens du Roi* advised another remonstrance, to which the magistrates agreed.[20]

By working rapidly de Mesmes was able to present his protest to the Regent the very next day. The Parlement hoped to obtain the return of the three exiles through the good will of the King. Moreover, the court had been extremely faithful to its duty, and anyone who thought otherwise was an enemy of the state, the King, and the Regent. The Regent replied only that everything depended on the conduct of the Parlement.[21]

The Interim Chamber, the group which remained during the holidays of the full court, continued the effort.[22] On September 22 its president, Maupeou, went to the Palais Royal with still another remonstrance on the absent magistrates. The Interim Chamber had been authorized by the full Parlement to make the most energetic attempts to obtain freedom for the exiles. Honor demanded it. The Regent was again asked either to free the magistrates as innocent or deliver them to the Parlement as guilty to be punished for their crimes. The document was only

[20] "Registres du conseil secret de Parlement de Paris," A.N., série X (1A) 8435, fol. 654, September 5, 1718; "Minutes du conseil secret de Parlement de Paris," A.N., série X (1B) 8900, item 13, September 5, 1718.

[21] Text is in Flammermont (ed.), *Les Remontrances,* I, 118–20.

[22] "Registres du conseil secret de Parlement de Paris," A.N., série X (1A) 8435, fol. 698, September 13, 1718; "Minutes du conseil secret de Parlement de Paris," A.N., série X (1B) 8900, item 38, September 13, 1718.

one sentence long. Like its predecessors, it was ineffective. The Regent could hardly free the exiles if the Parlement intended to punish them, so he replied as before that the whole affair was a matter of state.[23]

But Maupeou did not give up. Anxious to show the full session some results, he made one more attempt before the Interim Chamber closed. On October 21 he presented a new remonstrance, which was also very short. The Parlement had heard that the Regent might release the captives. The court hoped this meant that the search into the conduct of the magistrates had demonstrated their innocence. Might the Regent exercise clemency and allow the prisoners to go before the full sessions began? To this the Regent made an equivocal answer. The Parlement was regaining favor with the crown, but the conduct of the three exiles had been reprehensible. He blandly remarked that he would ask the eight-year-old-King if they ought to be released.[24] The Regent, a man of presence, performed the entire act with a straight face.

But the end was in sight. On December 19 the two councilors were released; Feydeau de Calende was liberated outright and returned to Paris, while Saint-Martin was ordered to his estate in Poitou. President Blamont remained in exile, and no mention was made of his fate. The issue was nearly resolved. Anticipating success, the Parlement decided to make one more remonstrance. On December 10 de Mesmes presented the fifth, and last, of this series of petitions. The Parlement first thanked the Regent for allowing Feydeau to return and Saint-Martin to live on his estates. But this was not enough. Saint-Martin ought to be able to return to Paris, and Blamont

[23] Text is in Flammermont (ed.), *Les Remontrances,* I, 121.
[24] *Ibid.,* I, 122–23.

should be freed. When the Parlement was established, the King had given it the right of judging its own members, a privilege which the court valued highly. The arrest of the three judges had been a serious blow to the prestige and position of the Parlement. The document ended with flattery, urging the Regent to listen to the voice of his heart and believe the Parlement completely submissive to him. The Regent equivocated. The arrests had not been made in anger, but for reasons of state. At present war with Spain was an imminent possibility. Things were troubled. No more could be done. If Blamont were guilty, he would be turned over to the Parlement; if innocent, he would be freed.[25]

It would, of course, have been no problem to concoct a case against the president and ruin him forever. But what purpose would it serve? Prince and court could never work together again. So Blamont was liberated, in stages. Toward the end of January he was allowed to leave the Iles d'Hyères and return to his estates. On May 15, 1719, Blamont was permitted to take his seat in the Parlement, and the court voted thanks to the Regent for his clemency.[26]

But the unfortunate Blamont was not the same man who had been exiled. His punishment had broken him, and his career as a young Turk was over. He became a spy for the Regent, reporting all that went on in the Parlement, but was soon found out and became a pariah,

[25] *Ibid.*, I, 124–26; Dangeau, *Journal*, XVII, 415; Saint-Simon, *Mémoires*, XXXV, 319–20; "Registres du conseil secret de Parlement de Paris," A.N., série X (1A) 8436, fols. 7–10, December 5, 1718; "Minutes du conseil secret de Parlement de Paris," A.N., série X (1B) 8900, item 9, December 5, 1718.

[26] "Registres du conseil secret de Parlement de Paris," A.N., série X (1A) 8436, fols. 363–64, May 15, 1719.

looked upon with horror by his colleagues. His friends fell away, and few cared to approach him. He resigned active occupancy of his office in 1726, and it passed out of his family at his death.[27]

---

[27] Bluche, *L'Origine des Magistrates*, 187; Marais, *Journal et Mémoires*, I, 442; Saint-Simon, *Mémoires*, XXXVI, 110.

CHAPTER VII

The Gallican Liberties: A Reprise

FOUR DAYS IN August had seen a *lit de justice* and exile for three magistrates. The collapse of the Parlement's political position had been abrupt and spectacular, but it was not an isolated event. The fortunes of the Parlement were part of the general tide of Regency politics, which underwent a profound upheaval during 1718. Not only did this occur with the court, but within the Council of Regency and in the finances and foreign policy as well. The tentative moves of the Regent's first two years had now either hardened or been discarded, and in all aspects of public life the regime acquired a sense of purpose and direction. The Regent was beginning to feel himself in possession of the answers to his problems of policy and personnel.

Although a bureaucratic state had been organized by the Sun King, politics had remained intensely personal. Relationships of family, tradition, and connections still exercised an immense influence on political figures. State decisions had personal repercussions, and rare was the minister or advisor who could survive a change of policy. Thus it was with the Parlement. In happier times the magistrates had been welcome at the Palais Royal, and their advice had been heeded. Although the Parlement remained outwardly unchanged, and no one lost his office, the *lit de justice* meant new personal and extra-institutional relationships between the individual magistrate and the royal ministers and officials. The defeat of the Parlement was part of a major shift in the personnel and focus of power of Regency politics. There now arose a triumverate of John Law, Father Dubois, and Marquis Argenson.

The influence of the *parlementaires* in the councils of the Regency had been diminishing for some time. On January 28, 1717, Chancellor Henri François d'Aguesseau was disgraced and exiled to his estate at Fresnes. Aguesseau, a member of a distinguished robe family, had been made chancellor in February, 1717, and had held the seals during the year of the court's greatest political prosperity. Because of his marriage into the important magisterial clan of Lefevre d'Ormesson, his personal friends were magistrates. He received their private advice as well as conceding to their public remonstrance. He was sympathetic to the constitutional position of the Parlement and esteemed its traditions. Disliking novelties or abrupt and sudden actions, in particular the economic theories of John Law, he showed a lawyer's love for precedent and calm reflection. All of this was evident in his considerate dealings with the Parlement.[1]

A year with the seals had amply demonstrated that Aguesseau's virtues were less and less to the taste of the Regent. Far different was his successor, Marquis Argenson. A hard man, who thought instinctively of force of arms, he had been lieutenant-general of the police of Paris. In this capacity he had run afoul of the Parlement

[1] See Bluche, *L'Origine des Magistrates,* 65–67, for a genealogical outline of the Aguesseau family. See Balteau, Barroux, and Prévost, *Dictionnaire de Biographie Française* (Paris, 1933–61), I, cols. 827–34, for a description of Aguesseau's career.

on several occasions, and in the Pommereu affair in 1717 the court had tried to seize and prosecute him.[2] The attempt failed, but the Parlement had not gained a friend. He had been chosen to succeed Aguesseau because of his unremitting firmness, his acceptance of whatever John Law might choose to do, and his total commitment to strong, efficient government. From the time of his elevation to the position of the Keeper of the Seals, Argenson argued that a reduction of the Parlement was absolutely necessary. For a long while the Regent had not taken the politics of the court too seriously, but its opposition to Law, and the urging of Argenson, had convinced him. The hard minister relished nothing more than humbling his old and persistent enemy.

The change in Regency politics extended to the finances as well. Here the influence of the traditional and conservative financial interests was on the wane. The funding of the bills of state and the Chamber of Justice had failed to provide a solution to the fiscal problems. The Parlement's dream of retrenchment of expenses and payment of obligations was simply impossible. The Duke of Noailles, a moderate man, had received his advice and ideas from the orthodox financial interests and as a result rapidly lost favor. In January, 1718, as soon as he heard of the disgrace of his political ally Chancellor Aguesseau, he resigned from the Council of Finances. Although personally fond of the duke, the Regent was not sorry to

[2] The Pommereu affair concerned the fate of a police spy, Pommereu, who had been arrested by the Parlement. When Argenson, the lieutenant-general of the police, intervened to save his employee, the Parlement threatened to arrest him as well. A direct order from the Regent was needed to quash the court's investigations, which were ended in very bad grace. Neither Argenson nor the magistrates ever forgot.

see him go, for he planned to follow the advice of the second triumvir, John Law. Noailles' replacement was none other than Argenson.

Although he was still only a foreign banker, Law's rise to influence did not go unnoticed by the established financial interests. Law's incipient system, at this stage composed of the bank and the Company of the West, was attacked during 1718 by a consortium of tax farmers led by Paris-Duvernay. They formed an antisystem and sold shares, just as did Law, but the shares of the antisystem were based on the known revenues of the Lambert Lease on the general farms, whereas Law's shares were based on the hope of Louisiana commerce. Attached to the antisystem were such *parlementaires* as President Dodun, a member of the Council of Finances and the scion of a financial family. During the recoinage protests, the Parlement had asked the advice of the bankers of the antisystem, who were in complete agreement that Law was a dangerous maniac. The court had attempted to reverse the trend of Law's growing influence by ordering the bank reduced to its original functions but had no success. The *lit de justice* was primarily a triumph for John Law, and the beginning of the end for the antisystem.

The personnel and structure of foreign policy were also undergoing a tremendous change in 1718. The Regent had early decided on peace and looked to an English alliance to ensure it. Entrusted to Father Dubois, this mission, after long and tortuous negotiations, had ended successfully in July, 1718, with the Triple Alliance between France, Great Britain, and Holland. Such a diplomatic victory vaulted Dubois into the inner councils of his prince and made him the third triumvir.

This foreign policy reversal to an anti-Spanish alliance

had not gone well everywhere. The Regent's advisors on the Council of Foreign Affairs, Villars, Vrillière and Armenoville, had been dubious about it from the start, as had Noailles and Aguesseau. The Duke of Maine and Marshal Villeroy, both on the Council of Regency, opposed it bitterly. The magistrates, drawn in by their friends and patrons in the ministry, were also opposed, particularly de Mesmes, a strong supporter of the Duke of Maine. Moreover, Philip V of Spain still nursed fantastic ambitions of becoming the Regent of France and instructed his ambassador, the Prince of Cellemare, to organize whatever opposition there might be to the Duke of Orléans. There was some. Centering around the circle of the Duke of Maine, and including the First President, a small group of lighthearted fools began the Cellemare Conspiracy against the Regent. All of 1718 was spent at this activity, with very little progress. Dubois and the Regent soon knew about it, and Dubois began to collect the evidence. The first move was made at the *lit de justice*. The Duke of Maine was reduced in rank and subjected to public humiliation. Marshal Villeroy, a friend of the Duke of Maine, was replaced as governor of young Louis XV by the loyal Duke of Bourbon. In September the Regent appointed his friend Claude le Blanc as minister of war, eliminating Marshal Villars and the inefficient council. Marshal Huxelles was replaced by Dubois as foreign minister. Having prepared for everything, in December the Regent arrested the rosewater conspirators, all of whom promptly turned state's evidence. De Mesmes he badly frightened, hinting dark treason at an interview. The political influence of the Parlement was one of the victims of the conspiracy that failed.

The change in Regency policies and personnel was

complete by the end of 1718. The Parlement lost its
friends within the inner circles of the Regent's friends
and advisors. Noailles, Aguesseau, Villars, and the magistrates on the councils all departed. Into their places
came the new triumverate—John Law, Father Dubois,
and Marquis Argenson. All three were on bad terms with
the Parlement, and all three found their personal and professional friends in men who disliked the pretensions of
the court. In every area their political ambitions and
ideas had been blocked and opposed by the magistrates.
They owed their present eminence to the favor of the Regent. Law, a Scotsman, Dubois, the son of a chemist, and
Argenson, for twenty years a minor official under Louis
XIV, had no independent power base, no personal wealth,
no cadre of influential friends. Their interests, connections,
and policies were all centered on the government of the
Regent.

Only one area of politics escaped the general reversals
of 1718. This was religion. Although Clement XI had
resumed confirming bishops for the vacant French sees in
April, relations between France and the Holy See had
remained poor. With all his other business the Regent
had had neither time nor energy to seek a religious settle-
ment. Nor had Father Dubois, busy with foreign affairs,
been able to advise in matters of Church government.
He had not yet obtained the necessary credit with his
prince to be entrusted with such a delicate matter. He
clearly saw, however, that in the end victory would have
to go to the ultramontanes, a view that he was to press
with increasing vigor upon his master; but, for the eighteen months after the *lit de justice*, the Regent was too
busy with the finances to listen to him. Thus the *lit de*

justice had no immediate effect on the struggle between the Gallicans and the ultramontanes.

The magistrates soon discovered that religious politics were still allowed them. The Regent was not dogmatic. He used his victory to end only the political activity he had not liked. Politics itself was not forbidden, merely because it was being practiced by a Parlement which had just been humiliated. The Regent was not greatly concerned with religion; therefore, the Parlement might be. The magistrates' political oblivion was not total at all, but selective. The Regent acted as if the *lit de justice* and the exile of the magistrates were not blows at the source of the Parlement's power, or even attempts to determine exactly the constitutional limits of the court's prerogatives. While it was certainly Argenson's opinion that the Parlement had been completely crushed, the Regent did not think so. No legal limits were placed on the functions and powers of the Parlement. The purpose of the *lit de justice* was to remind the magistrates to use those functions and powers as the Regent wished.

This only became clear with a renewal of political activity by the Parlement. It happened almost immediately. The signal for controversy came from the Pope himself. Clement XI, feeling the beginning of old age, decided that he had to act to end schism on his bull *Unigenitus.* He had watched the Gallican proclivities of the Regency government for nearly four years, hoping for a change. He had shown his good will and had even resumed sending bulls to consecrate French bishops, but there had been no apparent change in the Regent's opinions. Therefore, Clement decided to use the considerable power of his office to force all clerics at least to accept *Unigenitus.* On September 8, 1718, he published a de-

cree, *Pastoralis Officii,* ordering all the faithful to accept
the bull *Unigenitus* or have the church take disciplinary
action against them. The decree further declared that
prelates who did not accept the bull would be cut off from
communion with Rome. The papal nuncio presented the
document to the Regent, stressed its importance, and
urged him to act vigorously against the religious dissenters
in France.[3]

For an affair as important as a papal decree, the Regent
called the *gens du Roi* from their vacations. On their
return to Paris they conferred and tentatively recommended that *Pastoralis Officii* be appealed to the Parlement by a writ of error, if the Regent wanted to trust
such an important matter to the recently disgraced court.[4]
The Regent hesitated and then agreed. The Parlement
would be explicitly invited to re-enter the political arena.
On October 3 the papal decree was considered by the
Interim Chamber, which had been preoccupied with the
exiled magistrates. The new advocate-general Chauvelin
demanded suppression of *Pastoralis Officii.* He maintained
that no one could mistake the real reason for the papal
demand that the bull *Unigenitus* be accepted by the faithful. It was the notion of papal infallibility. While such
ideas might be strong in Rome, they were contrary to the
laws of France and even to the ancient canonical ways.
The magistrates had the clear duty to suppress the papal
decree. With such advice, and confident that the Regent
would approve, the magistrates could not refuse, and the
papal decree was suppressed forthwith.[5]

[3] Carreyre, *Le Jansénisme,* II, Pt. 1, p. 48; Dangeau, *Journal,* XVII,
385.

[4] Lamoignon, "Journal historique," 288–91; Dangeau, *Journal,* XVII,
397.

[5] Barthelémy (ed.), *Gazette de la Régence,* October 3, 1718, 287–88;

So much for the Pope. The whole affair seemed to be over. The Regent went back to his work with John Law and his concern over possible war with Spain. The Parlement returned to appealing for the release of the exiled magistrates. But the Parlement's suppression had not lessened the impact of *Pastoralis Officii* on the clergy. The decree kept appearing in various parts of France as ecclesiastics read and distributed it. The Parlement, with the agreement of the Regent, felt compelled to act again. In January, 1719, the magistrates again suppressed *Pastoralis Officii* and forbade any cleric to receive or execute any papal bull or letter without the permission of the Parlement.[6]

Villefore, *Anecdotes ou Mémoires secrètes*, III, 147–49; Dangeau, *Journal*, XVII, 398; "Registres du conseil secret de Parlement de Paris," A.N., série X (1A) 8435, fols. 706–14, October 3, 1718; "Minutes du conseil secret de Parlement de Paris," A.N., série X (1B) 8900, item 1, October 3, 1718; "Arrest de la Cour de Parlement qui reçoit le procureur-general du Roy comme Appellant comme d'Abus d'un décret du Pape intitulé 'Sanctissimi Domini nostri Domini Clementis divina Provendentia Papae XI litterae ad universos Christi fideles datae adversus eos qui Constitutioni Sanctitatis suae quae incipit Unigenitus . . . debitam obedientiam praestare hactenus recusarunt aut in posterum recusaverint' qui ordonne les exemplaires en seront apportez au greffe de la Cour. Fait défenses de l'exécuter, vendre, imprimer, etc., et renouvelle des défenses de recevoir, publier, exécuter, vendre, imprimer etc., aucuns Bulles ou Brefs de la Cour de Rome sans Lettres Patentes du Roy, registrées en ladite Cour," B.N., série F 23672, October 3, 1718.

[6] "Registres du conseil secret de Parlement de Paris," A.N., série X (1A) 8436, fols. 96–100, January 10, 1719; "Minutes du conseil secret de Parlement de Paris," A.N., série X (1B) 8900, item 13, January 10, 1719, with enclosures; "Arrest de la Cour de Parlement qui déclare abusives les lettres ou Décret du Pape intitulé 'Sanctissimi Domini . . . recusaverint.' Fait itératives défenses de l'exécuter, vendre, imprimer, etc. Ordonne la suppression d' une Lettre de Général des Carmes. Fait défenses de recevoir ny exécuter aucunes Bulles ny Brefs de Cour de Rome ny pareillement aucuns Décrets, Récrits, Commissions, etc., soit en forme de lettre ou autrement des Généraux d'Ordre ou autres

Suppression of a papal decree clearly indicated the Regent's sentiments concerning the Gallican liberties and ought to have been a decisive victory over the ultramontanes and Jesuits. Crown and Parlement seemed united in defense of the Gallican traditions. But the Gallican victory was only on the surface. Doctrinal pressure from the Pope might not mean much to the Regent, who was essentially an agnostic, but it did to the clergy, most of whom were not. The papal decree made its way around France, passed in manuscript from cathedral to cathedral. The bishops and their clergy read the decree and approved of it, for an enormous majority were ultramontane and cared much more for the Pope than the Parlement. The Regent and his Parlement were acting in a vacuum. The clergy of France was simply overwhelmingly in favor of the bull *Unigenitus,* and the Regent could not change this fact. The magistrates' notions of the Gallican liberties had no support in the French Church.

The Pope was aware of the vast support he had in the French Church and decided to reinforce the impression of *Pastoralis Officii.* In January, 1719, an edict from the Holy Office arrived in Paris which commanded denunciation to the Roman Inquisition of all Catholics who did not accept *Unigenitus* and *Pastoralis Officii.* Such action could not remain unnoticed, and the edict was soon handed to the *gens du Roi.* With the approval of the Regent, they brought it to the Parlement. The advocate-general, Lamoignon, maintained that the Holy Office edict commanded acceptance of the bull *Unigenitus* as an article of faith, which was contrary to the Gallican traditions. Having disposed of the edict, Lamoignon went on to

religieux étans hors le Royaume sans Lettres Patentes enregistrées de la Cour," B.N., série F 23672, January 10, 1719.

make a suggestion. In the present state of clerical unrest extra efforts had to be made to protect the liberties of France. It would be wise to forbid all regular clergy, who were decidedly ultramontane, from going to Rome without the permission of the King. The magistrates approved all of Lamoignon's suggestions.[7]

Seeing his success, Clement XI pressed his advantage. Determined to eradicate the last traces of Jansenist and Gallican opposition, he had the Inquisition issue another decree, dated August 12, 1719, which reached Paris by the beginning of September. It condemned the Gallican pastoral instruction of Cardinal Noailles. The message was quite clear. Having issued general condemnations against the episcopal holdouts, Clement XI moved against individuals, starting with the most prominent. If Cardinal Noailles could be broken, the four bishops who had published the first appeal would cave in. For the beseiged Gallicans and Jansenists, and for the Regent as well, the moment of truth was approaching.

The cardinal was horrified at the papal action, as were the rest of the Gallicans. If a prince of the Church could be menaced by the Inquisition, then what could help the others? Unhappy at the prospect of excommunication or martyrdom, they bombarded their leader with petitions

[7] Carreyre, *Le Jansénisme*, II, Pt. 1, p. 57; Dorsanne, *Journal de la Constitution "Unigenitus,"* I, 449; "Arrest de la Cour de Parlement qui ordonne la suppression d'un Décret intitulé 'Editto speciale del S. Offizio' du 19 Décembre 1718 affiché et publié à Rome le 22 Décembre et qui fait défenses à tout Religieux de quelque Ordre, Société ou Congrégation qui ce soit de sortir du Royaume sans permission du Roy, mesme sous prétexte d'aller aux Chapitres Généraux ou Provinciaux de l'Ordre," B.N., série F 23672, January 26, 1719; "Registres du conseil secret de Parlement de Paris," A.N., série X (1A) 8436, fols. 132–34, January 26, 1719; "Minutes du conseil secret de Parlement de Paris," A.N., série X (1B) 8900, item 42, January 26, 1719.

of complaint and help. The cardinal was in a difficult spot. An indecisive man at best, he was being literally torn apart. He did not want to go against his conscience or let the side down, and he could not meanly surrender. Yet open defiance of the Holy Father would put him in schism. With a nervous show of Christian moderation, he informed the Regent that if the papal decree were not suppressed, he would have to answer it and thus rekindle the doctrinal pamphlet wars and perhaps provoke a major breach with Rome.[8] No one wanted this. The Regent, still not completely ready to veer to the papal side, gave reluctant permission for an appeal to the Parlement. The cardinal appealed and easily won his case. On September 6 the Parlement suppressed its third papal decree in a single year.[9] The Gallicans were happy; the fortress was still safe, and the Regent's favor protected them.

If the Regent was prepared to defend the Gallican cause against the Pope, he could hardly fail to do so against one of his own bishops. Domestic as well as foreign enemies assailed the Gallican traditions. The papal decree *Pastoralis Officii* revived the ultramontane pamphleteers. The Parlement, without influence in the

[8] Dorsanne, *Journal de la Constitution "Unigenitus,"* I, 479; Dangeau, *Journal,* XVIII, 118.

[9] "Registres du conseil secret de Parlement de Paris," A.N., série X (1A) 8437, fols. 124–27, September 6, 1719; "Minutes du conseil secret de Parlement de Paris," A.N., série X (1B) 8901, item 26, September 6, 1719; Dorsanne, *Journal de la Constitution "Unigenitus,"* I, 479–80; Villefore, *Anecdotes ou Mémoires secrètes,* III, 177; Dangeau, *Journal,* XVIII, 119; Buvat, *Journal de la Régence,* I, 429; "Arrest de la Cour de Parlement qui ordonne la suppression d'un Décret de l'Inquisition de Rome du 3 Aoust 1719, portant condamnation de l'Instruction Pastorale de M. le Cardinal de Noailles," B.N., série F 23672, September 6, 1719.

finances, had plenty of time to detect and condemn domestic literature in support of the Pope. None of the papal pamphleteers was as vigorous, or wrote to such good effect, as the Bishop of Soissons, who soon became the constant concern of the magistrates.

Jean Joseph Languet de Gergy had been appointed Bishop of Soissons in 1715. He was an excellent diocesan administrator and soon found himself greatly admired for his liberality and kindness. A protégé of the great theologian and orator Jacques Benigne Bossuet, he followed his master in all things but Gallicanism. An unflagging polemicist, Languet became a zealous and irrepressible partisan of papal supremacy. He was particularly vocal about the continuing opposition to the bull *Unigenitus,* which he found to be perfectly acceptable. Although he disagreed with the Gallicans, Languet kept quiet until *Pastoralis Officii.* Then he started to publish. The Pope's enemies became his enemies. During the spring of 1719 he indulged in several violent polemics against the Gallicans, including the Parlement. His pamphlets were denounced in due course to the *gens du Roi,* who brought them to the court in May.[10] Lamoignon's comments were brief. He merely noted that the pamphlets had been published in defiance of the declara-

[10] Carreyre, *Le Jansénisme,* II, Pt. 1, pp. 166–67; Dorsanne, *Journal de la Constitution "Unigenitus,"* I, 460. The titles of the polemics are as follows: 1) "Avis aux Curez du Diocèse de Soissons donnez par Monseigneur l'Evesque au petit Synode du 30 Mars 1719"; 2) "Mandement du Monseigneur l'Evesque de Soissons au sujet de la Constitution 'Unigenitus' et de l'appel qui en a interjetté au futur concile" (December 8, 1718); 3) "Lettre de Monseigneur l'Evesque de Soissons à Monseigneur l'Evesque d'Angouleme au sujet de l'appel de ce Prélat et du Mandement qu'il a publié à Angouleme au Mois de Décembre 1718"; 4) "Lettre Pastorale de Monseigneur J. Joseph Languet, Evesque de Soissons, aux Ecclésiastiques de son Diocèse."

tion of October, 1717, which enjoined silence on religious issues. Nothing was said about the pamphlet's contents. In a brief, dignified speech, Lamoignon recommended suppression.

On this occasion, however, there was considerable debate. François Christophe de Bragelogne, one of the oldest and most influential councilors of the *Grand' Chambre*, defended the rights of bishops to regulate the spiritual affairs of their dioceses. After all, Languet was merely explaining the views of the Pope. As three of the four works in question fell into this category, they, at least, should not be suppressed. His argument was vigorously sustained by President Cochet de Saint-Vallier, a canon count of Brioude and the author of a celebrated treatise on the Indult.[11] But the ultramontane group in the Parlement was small. Father Pucelle, perhaps the leading Jansenist in France, urged that since Languet's pamphlets were derogatory to the authority of the King, the Parlement had a clear duty to suppress them. A powerful speaker with the advantage of addressing the prejudices of his listeners, he carried the court with him.[12]

Still dubious about the propriety of condemning the Bishop of Soissons without the express permission of the Regent, the magistrates did not suppress Languet's work immediately. They sent the *gens du Roi* to the Regent with the results of the debate. The procurer-general, Joly

[11] For data on Bragelogne and Saint-Vallier see Bluche, *L'Origine des Magistrats*, 107–108, 137. Melchior Cochet de Saint-Vallier, *Traité de l'Indult* (Paris, 1703).

[12] Buvat, *Journal de la Régence*, I, 389; Dorsanne, *Journal de la Constitution "Unigenitus,"* I, 460; "Registres du conseil secret de Parlement de Paris," A.N., série X (1A) 8436, fols. 367–68, May 16, 1719; "Minutes du conseil secret de Parlement de Paris," A.N., série X (1B) 8900, item 41, May 16, 1719.

de Fleury, a real diplomat, suggested that the whole irritating problem might be muted by reimposing the declaration of silence concerning the bull. Quite relieved, the Regent agreed. Having completed the document, Joly de Fleury next told his prince that the Parlement would balk at registering it until the publications of the Bishop of Soissons had been suppressed. Tolerant of such maneuvers, the Regent amiably agreed to present the new declaration of silence to the Council of Regency, where he supported it strongly.

After Pentecost Joly de Fleury brought his new declaration of silence to the Parlement. Apprehensive of royal displeasure, President Potier de Novion wished to discuss the declaration first, but the Jansenist Father Menguy felt that the court ought to attend to the Bishop of Soissons. Every councilor who followed him agreed. The *gens du Roi* were asked if they had changed their opinion about Languet's tracts. After a short consultation they declared the works abusive to the dignity of the Parlement, but they believed Joly de Fleury's new proposal would settle the problem. Consideration of this Delphic advice consumed the rest of the session, and it took two days to condemn the Bishop of Soissons and register the declaration of silence.[13] Even in the Parlement *Pastoralis Officii* was having its effect.

[13] "Registres du conseil secret de Parlement de Paris," A.N., série X (1A) 8436, fols. 387–88, June 6, 1719, fols. 389–91, June 7, 1719; "Minutes du conseil secret de Parlement de Paris," A.N., série X (1B) 8900, item 2, June 6, 1719, and item 4, June 7, 1719; Dorsanne, *Journal de la Constitution "Unigenitus,"* I, 460–63; Buvat, *Journal de la Régence,* I, 399; Dangeau, *Journal,* XVIII, 58–59; "Déclaration du Roy qui ordonne l'exécution de celle du 7 Octobre 1717 et suspend pendant un an toutes les disputes, contestations, et differends formez dans le Royaume à l'occasion de la Constitution de Nostre Saint Père le Pape

Languet was not fazed. A tenacious man with firm and fixed opinions, he neither gave nor asked quarter. Upon receipt of the news of the suppression of his tracts, he wrote more. He sent, and then published, a letter to the Regent. He attacked the declaration of silence, the authority of the King to make such laws, the order of the Parlement suppressing his tracts, and the powers of the Parlement in general.[14] Languet was a trenchant polemicist. In two vitriolic pages he roasted his enemies.

The letter shocked the Regent, who gave it immediately to the *gens du Roi*. On August 9 Lamoignon reported to the Parlement "that he was extremely disturbed at seeing printed and distributed in public a private letter, written to the Regent by a bishop of the Kingdom. While it is true the author of this letter begins by saying that he respects the Declaration of Silence of June, the first mark he gives of that respect is to break the silence it imposes so expressly. . . ." Lamoignon then defended the duty of the court to sustain the laws of the realm. He closed with the extremely Gallican statement that the ultramontanes would reduce the French bishops to spiritual dependence on the Pope.

These assertions appealed to the overwhelming majority of the magistrates and carried with almost no opposition. The Parlement ordered the letter to be burned and sent the lieutenant-general of Soissons to bring the court's

contre le Livre 'Réflexions morales sur le Nouveau Testament,' " B.N., série F 23622 (73), June 5, 1719; "Arrest de la Cour de Parlement qui déclare abusifs le Mandement de M. l'Evesque de Soissons du 8 Décembre 1718 et un avis de mesme Evesque de 30 Mars et qui ordonne la suppression de deux Lettres dudit Evesque," B.N., série F 23672, June 7, 1719.

[14] Text of the letter is in Carreyre, *Le Jansénisme*, II, Pt. 1, pp. 193–94.

decision to the bishop.[15] Languet was unimpressed. On August 15 he published his reply to the Parlement. It contained four sections, the most important of which denied the Parlement the right of preventing a bishop from saying what was necessary to the spiritual welfare of his diocese. This outraged the more Gallican magistrates, and they demanded that the contumacious bishop appear before the court.

The Regent categorically refused to do this. But the aggreived magistrates felt their honor impugned and demanded some action. When the Parlement met on September 4, 1719, the Gallican majority was angry. Father Menguy asked for immediate action against Languet and carried his colleagues with him. When the procurer-general brought his opinions in, they proved surprisingly harsh; Joly de Fleury had let his Gallican feelings run away with him. He recommended three steps—the first condemning the letter, the second ordering a fine of 20,000 *livres* to the hospitals of Soissons, and the third threatening much stronger punishment if Languet did not keep silence. The magistrates approved, but the Regent was not pleased with this proposal.

As the vacations started in three days, a series of hurried

[15] "Registres du conseil secret de Parlement de Paris," A.N., série X (1A) 8437, fols. 46–52, August 9, 1719; "Minutes du conseil de Parlement de Paris," A.N., série X (1B) 8901, item 11, August 9, 1719; "Arrest de la Cour de Parlement qui ordonne que l'Ecrit intitulé 'Lettre de M. l'Evesque de Soissons à S. A. R. M. le duc d'Orléans Régent du Royaume, au sujet de l'arrest rendu au Parlement le 7 Juin contre quelques Ecrits de cet Evesque' daté à la fin en ces termes, à Soissons le 24 Juin 1719, signé en ces termes, J. Joseph Evesque de Soissons, sera lacéré et bruslé par l'Exécuter de la Haute Justice et qui ordonne que ledit Evesque sera tenu d'avouer ou disavouer ledit Ecrit, l'impression et le publication qui a esté faite," B.N., série F 23672, August 9, 1719; Dorsanne, *Journal de la Constitution "Unigenitus,"* I, 471–72; Buvat, *Journal de la Régence,* I, 419; Dangeau, *Journal,* XVIII, 100.

conferences began. The Regent refused to accept Joly de Fleury's opinion, and the search for a compromise was initiated. The procurer-general toned down his conclusions, and the Regent gave in, allowing the case to continue. On September 6, the same day the Parlement suppressed the papal decree aimed at Cardinal Noailles, the court issued its order against the Bishop of Soissons, condemning him to pay 10,000 *livres* to the poor if he did not retract his letter in a week and threatening him with imprisonment.[16] The magistrates' objectives had been met. The Regent allowed a decision against Languet, and a rather strong one at that.

Languet, however, did not give up. He published a pastoral letter which raked the Parlement and denied its competence in these matters. Although the court was on vacation, Joly de Fleury took the letter to the Regent, complaining that it injured the honor of the Parlement. He suggested that Languet be really humiliated, but the Regent refused. Baffled but persistent, the procurer-general tried again in early November. He pleaded that a failure to act made a mockery of royal justice and added that the magistrates would surely investigate when the vacations ended. The Regent turned a completely deaf ear. Finally, an irritated Joly de Fleury engaged the First President and the two advocates-general to go with him to impress the prince with the gravity of the whole affair. De Mesmes complained that the Parlement had acted at the Regent's request and that the Regent was making a fool of everybody. To all their pressure the

[16] "Registres du conseil secret de Parlement de Paris," A.N., série X (1A) 8437, fols. 126–28, September 6, 1719; "Minutes du conseil secret de Parlement de Paris," A.N., série X (1B) 8901, item 27, September 6, 1719; Dorsanne, *Journal de la Constitution "Unigenitus,"* I, 478–82; Dangeau, *Journal,* XVIII, 119; Buvat, *Journal de la Régence,* I, 428–29.

Regent blandly replied that he worked for clerical peace and that any further action against the Bishop of Soissons would bring down the Pope.[17]

There it all ended. Audacity had succeeded, and the Bishop of Soissons had gained the Regent's protection. The Parlement's orders were not being enforced. What good would it do to issue new ones? Even Languet realized that the quarrel was over. Having had the last word, he showed moderation. He had scattered his enemies, and he was satisfied.

The magistrates were not satisfied, but there was nothing more they could do. All that was possible for the Gallican liberties had already been done. In the year from September, 1718, to September, 1719, the court had condemned nine ultramontane tracts, as many as in the remaining seven years of the Regency. The few Gallican bishops were getting as much support from the Parlement as they had any right to expect.

The Regent was the key. He was beginning to move away from the Gallican position. Increasingly under the influence of Father Dubois, he had swung toward the ultramontane view. The agnostic prince cared nothing for the doctrinal issues in question, which he hardly understood, and he had an amused and tolerant contempt for those who did. He did understand that his diplomatic relations with Rome were bad and that it was unnecessary for them to remain so. A Regency allied to a recent enemy and engaged in an unpopular war with Spain did not need gratutious foes. Relations with the Holy See could be improved easily, and it seemed only reasonable to improve them.

[17] Carreyre, Le Jansénisme, II, Pt. 1, p. 201; Dorsanne, Journal de la Constitution "Unigenitus," I, 484, 493–94.

The reasons for the quarrel seemed trivial. It might be argued that to a secular man all religious quarrels are trivial, but this one seemed so even by more rigorous standards of judgment. It was difficult to see how article 91 of the bull *Unigenitus* offended the Gallican liberties, and it was equally hard to understand how acceptance of the bull would lead to papal infallibility. Didn't the Regent appoint bishops and abbots regardless of *Unigenitus*? Couldn't he interdict communication with Rome in any case? Wasn't the *don gratuit* still paid to the crown? What difference did Jansenism, which was all but dead, make to anyone but the Pope? It left untouched the really important things about religion—the loyal hierarchy, the revenue, the support of the throne by the altar. Neither the Regent nor Dubois was an ideologist. They would not fight over nothing. By October, 1719, they had begun overtures of peace.

The final element in the Regent's slow evolution toward Rome was the utter weakness of the Gallican and Jansenist cause. Whatever its merits, if any, almost no one believed in them. A cardinal famed for his lack of discernment and four provincial bishops were all the Gallicans could muster. The rest of the hierarchy was either convinced or frightened by the Pope. Neither prince nor minister was unaware of the approval which the French episcopacy gave to *Pastoralis Officii*. Both concluded that it would be impossible to stir any breath of life into the Gallicans and foolish to try.

A final, important factor in the government decision to come to terms with the Papacy was the personal ambition of Father Dubois. The son of a country chemist, he had had the good fortune to become the future Regent's tutor and the good sense to win the prince's affection and confidence. An able statesman, he enjoyed increasing evidence of the Regent's trust. At the same time he fell under the suspicion of moral obloquy. Only a priest, without income or family, Dubois felt strongly the need to increase his personal stake in society. His particular goal was to become a cardinal, not an unreasonable ambition for a clerical minister. But the road to a red hat could be traveled only with the consent of the Pope, and Dubois clearly understood that this meant acceptance of *Unigenitus* by the Regent's government. This spurred his efforts, and Dubois found himself in the happy situation in which duty and ambition coincided perfectly. In October, 1719, therefore, Dubois and the Regent began to work on a formula which would satisfy the Pope and could be accepted by the Gallicans. At the same time, they halted the Parlement's suppression of ultramontane literature. And, for his part, on the strength of the changing dispositions of prince and minister, the Pope temporarily suspended his campaign against Cardinal Noailles.

All this was unknown to the magistrates. They merely saw the waning enthusiasm of the Regent for the Gallican cause as another evidence of the instability of a prince they were coming to think of as an enemy. If Dubois and the Regent were closing the religious quarrel, they were opening another area of conflict with the Parlement, but they did not care. Within the Regent's private councils policy was no longer made by men who had an eye for the Parlement.

CHAPTER VIII

John Law

THE REGENT OF France had always been genuinely concerned about the welfare of his people. He hoped to make the burden of government as light as possible, and to this end he was following the advice of his friend John Law in the belief that the financial advice he was receiving was wise and right. The Regent had enormous confidence in his ministers, and none stood higher than John Law. A personal friend as well as a financial advisor, the Scotsman had captivated his prince. Delighted with the promise and novelty of Law's system and impressed with his knowledge of fiscal matters, the Regent decided to put him in charge of the royal fiscal institutions, and as 1719 wore on, Law assumed more and more control over the royal finances.

John Law's economic theories were strange and wonderful for the early eighteenth century. He did not believe that a nation was wealthy in proportion to the gold and silver it held. He thought paper made better money than gold. He thought banks and easy credit were necessary to a proper functioning of the economy and maintained that low interest rates were better than high ones. Free trade was preferable to restrictions, and laws that hindered commerce simply impoverished the state and its people.

Law calculated that a nation's wealth was measured by

its total amount of trade and industry, creating a yardstick similar to the Gross National Product. In his economic theories Law was almost a Keynsian, but he was the only one. Orthodox mercantilist bankers and merchants were horrified at this economic heresy, at these dangerous novelties. The magistrates of the Parlement were also unconvinced. Most of the magistrates were fiscal conservatives, who neither understood nor accepted the new theories of credit and paper money. They had put their fortunes into land, office, and *rentes,* and they thought sound finance consisted of prompt payment of royal obligations. Law was a dangerous foreign lunatic who would ruin the state. Furthermore, they attributed the *lit de justice* of 1718 to Law's influence and thought that their company would not regain its lost prestige until Law was removed. He was a political enemy of the Parlement.

But there was nothing the Parlement could do. Law's bank was a success. As his notes were payable in fixed weight specie, they handsomely survived the recoinage crisis. Payable on sight, they had the confidence of the business and commercial community. Law had operated conservatively, and his notes were the only paper circulating at par. The bank was showing a profit. The Regent had every right to be impressed.

Pleased with the private bank, the Regent and Law were increasingly alive to the possibility of converting it into a royal institution. On December 4, 1718, the Council of Regency drew up an edict establishing in place of the private bank a royal bank with John Law as director. The notes of the new bank would be royal paper backed by the rather uncertain credit of the King. Law's personal prestige would help guarantee them. The profits would go to the treasury.[1] Although the magistrates of the Parlement at once conceived an immense dislike of the measure and asked that it be reconsidered, the Regent merely recast the edict as an order in council and published it without registration.[2] The venture began with the highest royal hopes and expectations.

The new bank worked nearly as well as the old. There was some suspicion of royal patronage, to be sure, but a good harvest and conservative management sustained the notes. The war with Spain during 1719 was the only cloud over the Regent's general optimism. Things even went well enough for the Regent and Law to think of expansion. In May, 1719, there appeared an edict joining the nearly defunct Company of the East Indies and China with the nearly defunct Company of the West. Law was to run both companies and finance their operations with the notes from his bank.[3] Law and his master were certain that this new colonization and trading venture would be an immediate and overwhelming success.

The Parlement was much less sure. In due course the edict had been sent to the Palais de Justice for registration, which the magistrates refused. Instead they named

[1] "Déclaration du Roy pour convertir la Banque générale en Banque royale . . .," B.N., série F 23621 (1021), December 4, 1718.

[2] "Registres du conseil secret de Parlement de Paris," A.N., série X (1A) 8436, fol. 24, December 12, 1718, fols. 31–32, December 16, 1718, and fol. 41, December 19, 1718; "Minutes du conseil secret de Parlement de Paris," A.N., série X (1B) 8900, item 23, December 12, 1718, item 37, December 16, 1718, and item 39, December 19, 1718; Dangeau, *Journal,* XVII, 437; Saint-Simon, *Mémoires,* XXXVI, 42; Buvat, *Journal de la Régence,* I, 346; "Arrest du Conseil d'Etat du Roy concernant la Banque royale," B.N., série F 23650, December 27, 1718.

[3] "Edit du Roy portant réunion des compagnies des Indes orientales et de la Chine à la Compagnie d'Occident," B.N., série F 23622 (68), May, 1719; Saint-Simon, *Mémoires,* XXXVI, 302–303.

commissioners to examine the edict.[4] After suitable delay the commissioners reported to their company that the edict ought not to be registered.[5] But it hardly mattered. The same day the court rejected registration, the Regent ordered the merger of the companies by an order in council.[6]

This plan succeeded as well as the last. The prevailing confidence radiated outward from Law and the Regent to the investing public. The royal banknotes were accepted as currency; in fact they were better, for they could not be devalued. Shares of the new Mississippi Company were purchasable with banknotes. As Law's fiscal administration had been sound, his management of the Mississippi Company inspired confidence, and after a brief period of doubt, the stock began to rise and the number of investors grew. Law seemed to have the golden touch.

Hopes and expectations soared. A huge speculation in the Mississippi stock occurred during the summer and fall of 1719. Instant paper fortunes were made in stock-jobbing in the unorganized and frantic curb exchange in the narrow Rue Quincampoix. At first the quotations merely rose every week, then each day, and then by the hour. Lackeys made thousands, the Duke of Bourbon

[4] "Registres du conseil secret de Parlement de Paris," A.N., série X (1A) 8436, fol. 385, May 26, 1719; "Minutes du conseil secret de Parlement de Paris," A.N., série X (1B) 8900, item 53, May 26, 1719; Dangeau, *Journal*, XVIII, 53.

[5] "Registres du conseil secret de Parlement de Paris," A.N., série X (1A) 8436, fols. 423–24, June 17, 1719; "Minutes du conseil secret de Parlement de Paris," A.N., série X (1B) 8900, item 30, June 17, 1719.

[6] "Arrest du Conseil d'Etat du Roy concernant la réunion des Compagnies des Indes orientales et de la Chine à la Compagnie d'Occident," B.N., série F 23651, June 17, 1719; Dangeau, *Journal*, XVIII, 64, 66.

millions. A valet sent to sell at a particular price delayed his transaction for lunch. An hour later the quotation had risen, and the servant pocketed his profit. In the tiny street thousands cursed and fought to buy and sell. Several were trampled to death. Cafe owners made fortunes. The Count of Horn, a relative of the Regent, murdered for some stock and was broken on the wheel for his efforts. A hunchback rented his hump as a writing desk and cleared hundreds of *livres* a day. Sedan chairs and bodyguards were at a premium, for no carriage could penetrate the mob of bawling, feverish humanity.

Shares surged forward hundreds of *livres* a day. The desparate temper of a gold rush gripped the speculators, and the number of investors increased until no more could enter the street. Almost all bought on margin, and few could sell for cash. But it didn't matter; the wealth of the Mississippi was boundless. Periodically, however, rumors swept the street and the market faltered. The price dropped dangerously. After a moment of shocked calm, there was a grim rush to sell and call margins. Hundreds were ruined, but the bulls, led by Law himself, rushed in to bolster the market, and the quotations were pushed even higher. By November, 1719, a single Mississippi share stood at 10,000 *livres*, 1,000 per cent of par. It never went higher, but such was the confidence in John Law that even the end of the great bull market only shaved the price of the stock.

At the same time the royal bank in the Rue Vivienne began to issue more notes to cover the rise in the value of the stock. Based first on hope, and then on faith, over two billion *livres* in notes were authorized by the dazzled Regent. The mob in the Rue Vivienne was exceeded only by that in the Rue Quincampoix. The banknotes not only sustained the inflation, they fed it, for they too were bought on margin. All of France did not contain two billion *livres* in specie.

The nation was rich, or thought it was. By some inexplicable magic John Law had discovered the philosopher's stone. He had made gold from paper and was busy distributing both to the people. The enlightened Regent was supporting this worthy project with all the authority the government possessed. Both Law and the Regent wallowed in public approbation. Eager to please and anxious for the public weal, both men seemed to have succeeded beyond their wildest imaginings.

The magistrates watched the success of the system with considerable interest. In the midst of universal confidence many were won over to John Law, but the Parlement as a unit did not soften its views. John Law must go, and the Regent return to the old ways of financial administration. Yet there was nothing the Parlement could do. During the inflation few wanted to hear any sniping at Law. The tremendous success of the system deprived the court of any moral or popular basis for opposition. Parisians certainly did not want to hear that Law was a maniac and that Mississippi was a bubble. Assurances and praise were more the spirit of 1719. Who would oppose wealth? Who would wish poverty? The magistrates held their peace.

In the giddiness of success much could be overlooked. Both the bank and the Mississippi Company went undisturbed by the Parlement. But John Law's economic theories were too radical for this truce to endure forever. In March, 1720, the quarrel broke out again over an issue which touched the magistrates very closely. By the spring of 1720 Law and the Regent were struggling manfully to bring the huge French fiscal machinery into line with the new theories. Law believed in low interest rates. An edict was issued reducing the interest rate on future *rentes* on the Hôtel de Ville from 5 per cent to 2 per cent.[7] This would cut down on the carrying charges on future government debt, make government paper a less inviting investment, and pump more money into the stock of the competing Mississippi Company. The Company was not so prosperous that it would refuse the investment of gold which normally went into the *rentes*.

Because of the Easter festivities, which went splendidly in 1720, the edict was not communicated to the Parlement until April 10, when it was read to the horrified judges. Vastly disturbed, they immediately named commissioners to draw up a remonstrance to the King.[8] Although they had allowed the most experimental and hazardous fiscal expedients to go unchallenged, the magistrates could not ignore a reduction of the interest rates on future *rentes*. This was a sacred royal obligation. Even a plan for a reduction of future interest greatly offended the magistrates and convinced them that the interest on existing paper would be reduced next.

[7] "Edit du Roy portant que les deniers qui seront cy-après donnez à constitution de rente par les sujets de sa Majesté ne pourrent produire par un an plus haut interest que celuy de denier cinquante," B.N., série F 23622 (200), March, 1720.

[8] "Registres du conseil secret de Parlement de Paris," A.N., série X (1A) 8437, fol. 379, April 10, 1720; "Minutes du conseil secret de Parlement de Paris," A.N., série X (1B) 8901, item 1, April 10, 1720; Dangeau, *Journal*, XVIII, 253–54; Flammermont (ed.), *Les Remontrances*, I, 126; Saint-Simon, *Mémoires*, XXXVII, 253–54; "Déclaration du Roy pour abolir l'usage des espèces d'Or au premier may prochain . . . pour abolir pareillement au premier aoust prochain l'usage des toutes les espèces d'Argent," B.N., série F 23622 (209), March 11, 1720. In an age of bullionism and mercantilism this was unheard of; it was the same as abolishing money.

On April 17, President Aligre led a delegation to the Palais Royal to present the remonstrance, a long and highly emotional protest. It began with the assertion that previous kings had never made such drastic changes in the interest rate at one blow. When the interest rate had been decreased, which was not too often, it had been done a little at a time, in order not to ruin the subjects without enriching the King. In 1665, Louis XIV had made the last reduction, to 5 per cent, and even this was not uniform over the whole kingdom, as the King feared to disrupt commerce. In spite of the many wars of his reign Louis never thought a reduction of the interest rate would help him.

The Parlement had hoped that the King knew of the sad state of the people and would do something about it. However, instead of correcting the financial situation, this new edict would merely add to the people's grief, and the court would be remiss in its duty if it did not report this fact. The consequences of the heaviest taxes could not approach the evil which would follow this edict. In one day an investor would be deprived of three-fifths of his income. He would be ruined without chance for recovery. The most faithful subjects had lent the King their specie and were being repaid in depreciated coin or paper for which they could find no use. Now their last resource was being taken from them. Investors would suffer more in six months of peace than they had in twenty years of war.

The prices of basic commodities had risen considerably as a result of the continued flux of money. Hoarding, always forbidden by the King, was becoming quite common. The magistrates had felt themselves unable to act, believing that excessive prices were better than no goods at all, but this new edict would only make the situation worse, to the great suffering of all the people. Domestic servants would be thrown out of work and would starve. Good and useful men would lose their fortunes. Fathers of large families would not be able to provide sustenance or education for their children. Many would have to use up their capital to exist. And all these ruined families would be useless to the state. Taxes would diminish, homes would be abandoned, universities would empty. People would no longer be able to pay the pensions of girls who became nuns, and marriages would fall off for lack of proper dowries. Children would be without education in their youth and without wealth in their majority.

It was true that the edict pertained to the future only and left present *rentes* untouched. But this was a vain appearance, for the crown would soon fund all of its obligations under the new rate. All the magistrates would thus be ruined, and the Parlement knew this would alarm the King. But this was not what worried the Parlement the most, for ". . . we would not be fit for the magistrature if we were not able to sustain ourselves in poverty with courage. . . ." It was the glory and interest of the King which motivated the Parlement, for one could not detach the interest of the sovereign from that of his people. The nation was a family with the King at its head, and he could not fail to attend to the misery of his people. Would future commerce be able to support itself on such a low rate of interest? Was the King insensible to the position of investors? They too were subjects of the King, and it was to the interest of the King not to reduce their fortunes. The document ended by asking the King to retract the edict.[9]

[9] Text of the remonstrance is in Flammermont (ed.), *Les Remontrances,* I, 126–39.

The remonstrance was wretched, by far the worst produced by the Parlement during the Regency. It told a long tale of domestic grief and hardship which was certain to follow a reduction in interest rates on bonds not yet issued. Skipping lightly over the fact that the reduction concerned future issues only, the magistrates produced their heartrending epic of the evil which would befall *rentier* families. It was difficult to see how all these hideous disasters could arise from the edict in question, and the remonstrance gave no clue as to why the *rentiers* must be bankrupted. Their present income was untouched, and buying *rentes* was voluntary.

In addition to all this, the magistrates did not inform the Regent of the real disadvantages of his edict. How could the crown persuade people to buy *rentes* at such a low rate of return? Those with money to invest would put their cash elsewhere. The new issues would, and later did, sell at great discount. Further, the edict had the serious psychological effect of advertising the fact that the crown's financial position was not all it might be. The edict made sense only if the crown were going to abandon the expedient of raising money by the sale of *rentes*. The remonstrance stated none of this. As a protest it was worse than useless; it was ridiculous.

The Regent and Law did not take the contents of the remonstrance very seriously. They assumed that the magistrates had acted out of self-interest in anticipation of an assault on the present interest rate. Although the magistrates had stated that they could bear poverty with courage, it was clear that they much preferred to remain rich. Neither Law nor the Regent thought that anyone would pay much attention to so esoteric a question as interest on future *rentes* as long as the Mississippi shares stayed high. But the fact of a remonstrance was another matter and deserved some consideration. It meant the end of the long parlementary respite from financial politics and the start of a new attack on Law and his system. Such a development should not be ignored. Profits from Mississippi were not so great that critics could be encouraged. Law himself wrote a pamphlet rebutting the arguments advanced in the remonstrance.[10] The Regent also acted. On April 22 he ordered immediate registration of the edict on interest rates without further discussion.

Both belligerent and unhappy, the magistrates decided on further resistance. With only a single dissent, that of Bragelogne, they decided not to register the edict, but to make a new remonstrance.[11] This proved to be impossible. On May 3 the *gens du Roi* told the Parlement that the Regent was not going to hear any new remonstrance on the interest rate. In any case, the *gens du Roi* told the court, the Regent had already published the edict as if it were registered. The discussion was closed. But the magistrates were not intimidated. After hearing the dismal report of the *gens du Roi*, they delayed registration, and, by a vote of 97 to 27, decided to ask the Regent to hear a new remonstrance.[12] The prince merely re-

[10] John Law, *The Present State of the French Revenues and Trade, and of the Controversy betwixt the Parlement of Paris and Mr. Law* (London, 1720).

[11] "Registres du conseil secret de Parlement de Paris," A.N., série X (1A) 8437, fols. 413–14, April 22, 1720; "Minutes du conseil secret de Parlement de Paris," A.N., série X (1B) 8901, item 30, April 22, 1720; Dangeau, *Journal*, XVIII, 272; Saint-Simon, *Mémoires*, XXXVII, 255; Flammermont (ed.), *Les Remontrances*, I, 139–40.

[12] "Registres du conseil secret de Parlement de Paris," A.N., série X (1A) 8437, fol. 445, May 3, 1720; "Minutes du conseil secret de Parlement de Paris," A.N., série X (1B) 8901, item 1, May 3, 1720.

ferred the Parlement to the publication of the edict. What point was there in protesting a law already in effect? The Parlement did not renew its attempt to remonstrate. Things were calming down.

Neither John Law nor the Regent was as calm about the financial situation as he seemed, however. In spite of the brusque rejection of the Parlement's complaints and the seeming success of the system, both of them were uneasy about the Mississippi Company and the bank. Colonization in the lower Mississippi was much more expensive than had been imagined, and profits from trade were much less than had been anticipated. No gold or silver had been found. Although Law's bank held the farm of the indirect taxes, even this immensely valuable concession did not cover the carrying charges on the royal debt, which the bank had also assumed. On top of this was the bank paper, presumably covered by gold. Finally, both Law and the Regent felt that the Mississippi shares were selling above their true worth. As neither was inclined to minimize the value of the stock, this estimate was not a wild guess.

Since nothing could be done about the machinery of tax collection or the lack of bullion in the lower Mississippi valley, the Regent decided to lower the stock quotation. On May 21 he issued an edict reducing the price of the shares of the Mississippi Company. They were to be lowered in price 500 *livres* a month, until December, 1720, when they would sell for 5,000 *livres*. This would be a reduction of half, yet the shares would still be 500 per cent of par. This gradual deflation would also apply to the banknotes from Law's royal bank.[13]

[13] "Arrest du Conseil d'Etat du Roy concernant les Actions de la Compagnie des Indes et les Billets de Banque," B.N., série F 23651, May 21, 1720; Buvat, *Journal de la Régence*, II, 85–86; Dangeau, *Journal*, XVIII, 291; Saint-Simon, *Mémoires*, XXXVII, 314–15.

Whatever the fiscal merits of this decision, it was a psychological disaster. It was obvious to all that the crown itself, which had the biggest stake in the success of the Mississippi Company and the bank, was admitting that the shares and notes were inflated by half. What was their true value? Were they merely inflated by half, or by much, much more? Every investor leaped to the latter conclusion. Panic, immediate and enormous, as grim and ferocious as the previous inflation had been, swept over the investors. Margins were called on every hand. Everyone who was the least bit overextended was ruined. Previously, there had been no limit to buying on credit; now everyone wanted his money in specie. But Gresham's Law drove the specie into vaults and mattresses, and only paper circulated, at huge discount. The notes and shares collapsed overnight. Fortunes disappeared, and men who had bought paper fought to sell at the most ruinous loss. "No one of wealth who does not believe himself ruined . . . no one poor who does not see destitution . . ." was the dry comment of Saint-Simon.[14] On May 25 there was a riot in front of the bank, and stones were hurled at the building. Paper was refused in the markets. The Regent called out the troops to maintain order.

The magistrates felt that they could not lose so favorable an opportunity to tell the Regent that they had been right about Law all along. He really was a dangerous maniac, and the magistrates had known it from the beginning. The Parlement met on the morning of May 27 to discuss what ought to be said and done. It was decided that an immediate remonstrance should be made to the King. In the middle of the discussion, however, the Parle-

[14] Saint-Simon, *Mémoires*, XXXVII, 314–15.

ment received a clear indication that the Regent's attitude toward the court had undergone considerable change during the last week. He no longer felt that he should show lofty indifference to the magistrates. He would treat them with consideration. At noon on the twenty-seventh, Marquis Vrilliere appeared at the Palais de Justice to tell the court that the Regent had annulled the edict of May 21 which had started the panic. The new edict restored the notes and shares to their previous value.[15] The magistrates were duly gratified at this example of royal confidence.

But the new edict did nothing to restore confidence in the notes and shares. They continued to fall as fast as buyers could be found. Law's paper circulated at increasing discount. Street vendors even refused to accept it. In the midst of this catastrophe the Regent did the best he could. On May 29 he dismissed Law as Comptroller-General of the Finances, a move which was much applauded. The Parisians attributed this to the firmness of the Parlement. The crash convinced Paris that the magistrates had been right from the beginning, a view which the Parlement shared; and the reputation of the Parlement rose as the shares fell.

The fantastic velocity of the panic, the constant stream of bad news, the increase of criticism and vituperation—all this unnerved the Regent. He had borne up well

[15] "Registres du conseil secret de Parlement de Paris," A.N., série X (1A) 8438, fols. 14–16, May 27, 1720; "Minutes du conseil secret de Parlement de Paris," A.N., série X (1B) 8901, items 60–61, May 27, 1720; Barbier, *Journal historique et anecdotique,* I, 27; Dangeau, *Journal,* XVIII, 294–95; Saint-Simon, *Mémoires,* XXXVII, 319; "Arrest du Conseil d'Etat du Roy qui révoque celuy de 21 mai concernant les Actions de la Compagnie des Indes et les Billets de Banque," B.N., série F 23651, May 27, 1720.

under personal unpopularity, but the sudden and unexpected collapse of the system from which he had anticipated so much good left him at sea. He did not understand why the system had failed, and no one else did either. He could find no one to give him advice. Bewildered and tired, he wanted to do the right thing, but he did not know what it was.

In all the confusion the Regent fell back on the policies with which he had begun his reign. He began to conciliate the now popular Parlement. On June 8 there was a conference on the finances at the Palais Royal, attended by five deputies of the Parlement and M. le Peletier des Forts, the new Comptroller-General of the Finances. They discussed both the crash and the crown's insatiable need for money, but general agreement was impossible. Neither side wished to appear guided by the other, and no one really trusted anyone else, but a palliative was finally accepted. Twenty-five million *livres* in *rentes* at 2½ per cent, which could be bought in paper, were to be issued. It was hoped that this would avert a total crash and restore confidence in government paper. How investors could be persuaded to buy *rentes* at an unattractive rate in a period of extreme deflation was not discussed. Nor was there any indication that offering *rentes* for paper clearly showed the worthlessness of both. But the magistrates approved, and by a unanimous vote the Parlement registered the edict.[16] The new *rentes* did not sell very well. The Regent concluded that the public did not understand the terms of

[16] "Registres du conseil secret de Parlement de Paris," A.N., série X (1A) 8438, fols. 39–42, June 10, 1720; Dangeau, *Journal*, XVIII, 300–302; Marais, *Journal et Mémoires*, I, 272, 279–80; Saint-Simon, *Mémoires*, XXXVII, 335–36; "Edit du Roy portant création de vingt-cinq millions de livres des rentes au denier 40 sur l'Hôtel de Ville de Paris," B.N., série 23622 (256), June, 1720.

his generous offer to exchange worthless bonds for worthless paper and issued a clarification which liberalized the technical aspects of the edict. The magistrates agreed with the Regent's diagnosis and promptly registered his declaration.[17] Both were convinced that a sound beginning had been made in clearing away the fiscal debris.

This small manifestation of cooperation by no means reconciled the Parlement to its prince. The magistrates continued to grumble in public that they had been right all along, that they had recognized Law as a lunatic, and that the Regent really ought to take more notice of their financial wisdom. The harrassed prince told the Parlement's deputies to confer with the chancellor on the finances and leave him alone. But this did not satisfy the magistrates. On July 6 they sent another delegation to the Regent to complain about the lack of hard currency in Paris and to ask when the bank would reopen. Philippe d'Orléans curtly replied that he was doing the best he could. The magistrates returned after dinner to pester the Regent again. He had just settled down to his nightly six bottles of champagne with his cronies and was amazed and outraged to see the Parlement's deputies again. With some effort he retained his courtesy and promised that Paris would have money. Asked when, the exasperated Regent exploded, "Ah, when, when, when, I do not know! It is when I am able!" Then he threw the magistrates out.[18]

---

[17] "Registres du conseil secret de Parlement de Paris," A.N., série X (1A) 8438, fol. 82, June 22, 1720; "Minutes du conseil secret de Parlement de Paris," A.N., série X (1B) 8901, item 69, June 22, 1720; Marais, *Journal et Mémoires*, I, 301–303; Dangeau, *Journal*, XVIII, 307; "Déclaration du Roy concernant les rentes de l'Hôtel de Ville," B.N., série F 23622 (272), June, 1720.

[18] "Registres du conseil secret de Parlement de Paris," A.N., série X

Conferences with the chancellor, long suggested, now began. The Parlement sent deputies to consider remedies for the fiscal crisis. The chancellor, acting on orders from the Regent and Comptroller-General des Forts, proposed immediate registration of all orders in council concerning the bank and the Mississippi Company, attempting to associate the Parlement with the crown in the responsibility for the disaster. The court would register none and suggested instead an accounting of the specie in Law's bank. As there was no specie, the chancellor could hardly agree and muttered that the Parlement's sole contribution to the crisis had been to oppose everything the Regent tried to do. In reply the magistrates merely pointed to the huge state debt. Hearing this, Chancellor Aguesseau visibly brightened. He had three remedies for the state debt. First, the new *rentes* ought to be fully subscribed, which meant that the magistrates should purchase some. Next he proposed an open accounting of the notes issued by the bank, of which 600 million would be burned. Finally, the wealthy of the realm, including most of the magistrates, ought to subscribe among themselves a fund of another 600 million in paper to aid the state. Aguesseau added that he had thought to tax the rich, but that the experience of the Chamber of Justice had convinced him that they would not pay.

The Parlement's deputies were cool to the chancellor's proposals. They replied that the new *rentes* were badly undersubscribed, a situation of which Aguesseau was already aware. They next said that the open accounting

---

(1A) 8438, fols. 103–105, July 5, 1720; "Minutes du conseil secret de Parlement de Paris," A.N., série X (1B) 8901, item 18, July 5, 1720, Barbier, *Journal historique et anecdotique*, I, 34; Marais, *Journal et Mémoires*, I, 315–17; Dangeau, *Journal*, XVIII, 316.

was simply a pretext for taking the paper after having taken the specie and returning neither. As for the wealthy providing a fund, this did not seem feasible. What the Parlement asked was for Law to be dismissed from any control over the finances. Nothing less would do. Aguesseau brushed this aside, but the magistrates persisted, maintaining that while they had sacrificed their fortunes, they still had their honor and would not sacrifice that. With these recriminations the conference of July 13 ended. The deputies did promise, however, to bring to the Parlement the letters patent establishing the open accounting of the books of the bank.[19]

Three days later the magistrates and the chancellor met again. In the course of their conferences the deflation had continued at a terrific rate. The new issue of *rentes* had not seemed to help at all, and further remedies were needed. To this end the chancellor showed the deputies an edict transforming the Mississippi Company into a commercial venture which would reimburse the bank 600 million in the next year.[20] But the deputies were not convinced. Meeting to evaluate their sessions with the chancellor, the magistrates complained bitterly that all of the chancellor's proposals were bad. The public accounting of the bank notes was undesirable; taxation of the rich was even worse. The edict converting the Mississippi Company into a commercial institution was rejected out of hand. Finally, they felt that Aguesseau had been evasive. He had said that there was 2.2 billion in

[19] "Registres du conseil secret de Parlement de Paris," A.N., série X (1A) 8438, fols. 143–50, July 17, 1720; "Minutes du conseil secret de Parlement de Paris," A.N., série X (1B) 8901, item 58, July 17, 1720; Marais, *Journal et Mémoires*, I, 321–23.

[20] Marais, *Journal et Mémoires*, I, 327; Dangeau, *Journal*, XVIII, 322–23.

notes and later admitted that this might be in error.
The Parlement could accept nothing of the chancellor's
program.[21]

This did not please the Regent, although he had not
really expected much from the conferences between
Aguesseau and the Parlement. He had seen them as a
charade to keep the magistrates calm and occupied, but
he did not want to see the Parlement's opposition increase.
In July the Regent took the court's antagonism much more
seriously than he had before the crash. There were troops
in the street every day as a precaution against sedition
as much as to keep the bank and markets open. There
had been riots all over Paris. The Parlement might set
off another Fronde. On July 18 the Regent held a Council
of Regency to discuss the Parlement. After hearing from
his chancellor the unhappy details of the meetings with
the magistrates, the Regent announced that he was going
to exile the Parlement from Paris. Its opposition to the
crown had become unbearable, and good order demanded
some action. The entire council agreed with him. There
was deliberation only about the amount of force needed
to ensure the obedience of the magistrates. On July 19 and
20 the streets of Paris were filled with soldiers. Led by
their officers, they patrolled everywhere. The Parlement
was undisturbed, assuming that the troops were employed
in keeping mobs from Law's bank. But they weren't. They
were securing Paris for the departure of the Parlement.

[21] "Registres du conseil secret de Parlement de Paris," A.N., série X
(1A) 8438, fols. 143–50, July 17, 1720; "Minutes du conseil secret de
Parlement de Paris," A.N., série X (1B) 8901, item 58, July 17, 1720;
Saint-Simon, *Mémoires*, XXXVII, 355; Dangeau, *Journal*, XVIII, 322–23;
Marais, *Journal et Mémoires*, I, 328–29.

CHAPTER IX

Exile to Pontoise

AT FOUR O'CLOCK on the morning of July 21 the storm broke over the Parlement. Musketeers and their officers pounded at the doors of the magistrates. Each judge was roused from his bed and given a *lettre de cachet* ordering him to Pontoise, a small town about twenty miles from Paris. Standing sleepily in their dressing gowns, the magistrates read that they had forty-eight hours to leave for Pontoise, where the Parlement was to reassemble "to render ordinary justice." The officers demanded a written receipt stating that the judge had seen his letter and then departed into the morning haze, leaving their host to ponder impending exile.[1]

Between four and five that same morning the Palais de Justice was occupied by soldiers and closed to the Parlement. A sentry was stationed at the First President's door to prevent him from calling a meeting of the Parlement in his apartments. Soldiers also guarded the home of the chief secretary of the court, Gilbert de Voisins, to keep him from calling the court to meet anywhere. Finally, the Regent allocated 200,000 *livres* to pay for the magistrates' move, so that none might plead poverty in order to remain in Paris.[2] The Regent had grievous faults, but

[1] Marais, *Journal et Mémoires*, I, 324; Arthur de Marsy (ed.), *Le Parlement à Pontoise en 1720: Journal rédigé par un cordelier du couvent de cette ville* (Paris, 1863), 5.

[2] Dangeau, *Journal*, XVIII, 325.

pettiness was not one. He was also prudent and took every precaution to see that his orders would be carried out. He was obeyed. The magistrates began their move to Pontoise without disturbance.[3]

During the next two days most of the magistrates arrived at Pontoise. De Mesmes and his family were lodged by the Duke of Albret at his estate, a beautiful place with a garden by the river. The others did the best they could, finding rooms and suites with artisans and bourgeois, packed in like sardines. So great was the influx of *parlementaires* into the tiny town that the procurer-general had to write letters of requisition to thirteen surrounding villages to ensure food. While the magistrates were arriving, Gilbert de Voisins was looking for a place for the Parlement to meet. After much searching, he decided on the hall of the Cordeliers convent. Like the lodgings, it was none too good, and he had to send to Paris for the necessary furnishings. The magistrates, meanwhile, got settled, visited each other, or simply did nothing. Justice was suspended at the clients' expense.[4]

By July 27 the court had pulled itself together sufficiently to hold a short session. Everyone who could squeeze in attended. When called, the *gens du Roi* brought a declaration from the King ordering the Parlement to Pontoise. The document stated that the King was quite unhappy

[3] *Ibid.,* XVIII, 324–25; Marais, *Journal et Mémoires,* I, 332–34, 337–38, 352–55; Barbier, *Journal historique et anecdotique,* I, 40–42; Buvat, *Journal de la Régence,* II, 114–15; Saint-Simon, *Mémoires,* XXXVII, 360–62; Balleroy, *Les Correspondants,* II, 185; Jean-Gilbert Delisle, *Journal du Parlement séant à Pontoise depuis 21 juillet jusqu'à 11 novembre,* A.N., série U 747, pp. 2–3.

[4] Delisle, *Journal du Parlement,* A.N., série U 747, pp. 3–4; Saint-Simon, *Mémoires,* XXXVI, 363–65; Marais, *Journal et Mémoires,* I, 338.

to see that the officers who compose our Parlement of Paris, abusing the authority that we wish to give them, and forgetting that their sole duty ought to be to concur in the maintenance of ourselves in all our splendour, do themselves damage in prolonging the execution of our decisions on the administration of the finances of our Kingdom, and our intention being to prevent new difficulties on their part, which could produce no other effect than to sow defiance and trouble in our good Town of Paris, we have resolved to transfer our said Parlement of Paris to another town, where it will only be occupied in rendering justice to our subjects. . . .[5]

Since the Parlement was already in Pontoise, the *gens du Roi* asked for immediate registration. The magistrates agreed, adding that the Parlement would give "the customary service it has always rendered until now, with the same attachment and the same attention to the good of the State and the public that it has always [had], the said Court continuing to give the King the marks of the same fidelity that it had for his predecessors . . . from which it will never depart. . . ."[6] Once ensconced in Pontoise, the magistrates did as little work as possible. The lawyers licensed to plead before the Parlement met in Paris and decided not to come to Pontoise, nor to plead in another tribunal. Justice came to a complete halt. De Mesmes, who

[5] Isambert and others (eds.), *Recueil général*, XXI, 185–86; Marais, *Journal et Mémoires*, I, 352–53; Marsy (ed.), *Le Parlement à Pontoise*, 7–8; Lucien Perey, *Le Président Hénault et Madame du Deffand* (Paris, 1893), 540–42.

[6] Text of the edict is in Dangeau, *Journal*, XVIII, 328–29; see also Marais, *Journal et Mémoires*, I, 352–54; Marsy (ed.), *Le Parlement à Pontoise*, 8; Delisle, *Journal du Parlement*, A.N., série U 747, p. 5; "Registres du conseil secret de Parlement de Paris," A.N., série X (1A) 8438, fols. 163–64, July 27, 1720; "Minutes du conseil secret de Parlement de Paris," A.N., série X (1B) 8901, item 69, July 27, 1720.

was quite rich, filled in the long summer days as best he could. He entertained thirty to forty magistrates a day at his estate, feeding them at huge tables in the garden by the river. The other presidents followed as their purses allowed. This went on through July into August, turning the term of justice into an Arcadian festival. But no one complained.

Having got his Parlement to Pontoise, the Regent began thinking of ways to use it. Not needing justice, he turned to politics. He could, of course, have sent financial edicts to the court, but the collapse of Law's system had given him more pressing worries than the registration of edicts. Besides, in the face of total disaster, he had no idea what kind of financial edict he should produce, nor any confidence that it would be obeyed even if registered. But his problems with the Gallican liberties did not disappear because of the collapse of Law's system. And even if they had, Dubois, who wanted his red hat, would be there to revive them. Perhaps the exiled court could be pressured into registering an edict which would end disputes over the bull *Unigenitus*.

Since October, 1719, when the Parlement had condemned its last papal letter, the Regent and his minister had been working on a plan to close the clerical dispute. They silenced the Parlement's condemnations of ultramontane literature and drew up a conciliatory declaration which they had tried to make acceptable to all. By June, 1720, their effort had taken the form of letters patent on the bull which won the qualified acceptance of Cardinal Noailles, who promised to adhere to the document when the Parlement registered it. On August 4 the letters patent, now formally drawn up as an edict, were considered by the Council of Regency, and this final declaration was approved for submission to the Parlement.[7]

The declaration of August 4 began with a long preamble, stating the desire of the Regent for peace in the Church and indicating that the document had been approved by most of the episcopacy. The first article gave satisfaction to the Pope, stating that the bull, and its registration by the Parlement in 1714, would be executed and obeyed. No one could hereafter write directly or indirectly against the bull. The second article likewise soothed papal sensibility by forbidding any appeals to a future Church council. The Parlement was ordered to return to the bishops all judgment in matters of doctrine. The fifth article enjoined silence on everyone and forbade anyone to call his enemy a Jansenist, heretic, or schismatic. The declaration of August 4, a nearly complete ultramontane victory, maintained only the barest shred of Jansenist or Gallican honor, declaring that bishops might control their own dioceses in matters of doctrine. For the rest, it reflected accurately the huge weight of ultramontane opinion in the French clergy, the pressure from Rome, and the desires of Dubois for promotion.

On September 2 the declaration was sent to the court. For reasons not at all clear, Dubois and his master had procrastinated, waiting a month before the battle for registration. But once they moved, they meant to be obeyed, and thus they informed the *gens du Roi*. When Lamoignon read his opinions to the plenary session of the Parlement, he urged that the declaration be registered.

[7] "Déclaration du Roy touchant la conciliation des Evesques du Royaume à l'occasion de la Constitution 'Unigenitus,'" B.N., série F 23622 (321), August 4, 1720. Text can also be found in Léon Mention, *Documents relatifs aux Rapports du Clergé avec la Royauté de 1705 à 1789* (Paris, 1903), II, 52–60.

Joly de Fleury added his concurrence, calling for registration with very minor modifications.

Then came the discussion. Pallu, named reporter on the declaration, began to read it to the assembled magistrates but was quickly interrupted. Gabriel de la Porte announced to his colleagues that he had a sealed request from the four bishops who had made the first appeal to a future Church council.[8] De Mesmes cried an astonished protest that such an important document had not been sent to him and demanded that it not be read. De la Porte embarrassed the ultramontane First President into silence by asking him what would have happened to the request if it had been sent to him. Led by the indignant de la Porte, the magistrates demanded a vote on whether to read the bishops' request. This preliminary vote was the crucial test of registration. De Mesmes knew it and tried to postpone the division until he had had time to lobby, but he failed. By a vote of 70 to 48 the magistrates decided to read the bishops' letter. The Gallican majority, though slimmer than usual, was still secure, and when thirty commissioners were named to examine the declaration and all other pertinent documents, the committee was strongly Gallican.[9]

[8] The bishops of Senez, Mirepoix, Montpellier, and Boulogne.

[9] The bishops' request, and a similar one from the Sorbonne, contained a demand that the bishops be received by the Parlement as appellants by writ of error in all matters concerning the bull. Thus they asked prior agreement that all actions of the bishops who had accepted the bull could be appealed to the court. "Registres du conseil secret de Parlement de Paris," A.N., série X (1A) 8438, fols. 235–39, September 2, 1720; "Minutes du conseil secret de Parlement de Paris," A.N., série X (1B) 8901, item 1, September 2, 1720; Marais, *Journal et Mémoires,* I, 415, 423–24; Dorsanne, *Journal de la Constitution "Unigenitus,"* II, 16–17; Villefore, *Anecdotes ou Mémoires secrètes,* III, 213–15; Marsy (ed.), *Le Parlement à Pontoise,* 10; Delisle, *Journal du Parlement,* A.N., série U 747, pp. 21–23.

The commissioners began their meetings at once. Repairing to de Mesmes' estate, where he could watch them, they examined the declaration, the registration of *Unigenitus* in 1714, and all orders of the Parlement concerning the bull. They worked day and night. Nothing de Mesmes could say or do could erode the Gallican predisposition of the commissioners. It began to appear by the fifth that the commission was going to conclude in favor of rejection, or at least for modifications so substantial that the Regent would not accept them. This trend of events was very upsetting to Procurer-General Joly de Fleury, who had advised the court to register the declaration. He sent a courier to Paris to apprise the chancellor of the drift of events at Pontoise. Aguesseau, a strong partisan of order and royal prerogative, informed the Regent, complaining of the conduct of the Parlement, the bishops, and the Sorbonne.[10]

This jolted the Regent out of his pleasant delusions about the submissiveness of the Parlement. He sent Marquis Vrilliere with a *lettre de cachet* ordering immediate registration without modification. Vrilliere arrived at four-thirty on the morning of the seventh, went straight to the First President, and waked him. Confronting the startled man, the marquis showed him the letter. De Mesmes told him that the Parlement was to meet that morning and would vote on the declaration. He also assembled the thirty commissioners and had the marquis explain his mission once more. The commissioners replied that "registration pure and simple" was

[10] Delisle, *Journal du Parlement*, A.N., série U 747, pp. 25–26; Dorsanne, *Journal de la Constitution "Unigenitus,"* II, 17–18; "Registres du conseil secret de Parlement de Paris," A.N., série X (1A) 8438, fols. 257–59, September 5, 1720; "Minutes du conseil secret de Parlement de Paris," A.N., série X (1B) 8901, item 18, September 5, 1720.

not certain, as they themselves were going to recommend important modifications. In any case the Parlement as a whole would have to vote.

Later the same morning the Parlement met. The session was hostile. Vrilliere's proposal for simple registration had little support. The marquis then presented the court with his *lettre de cachet* demanding return of the declaration, since it had not been registered. Unanimously, the magistrates voted to obey the King, and the declaration of August 4 was handed to Vrilliere.[11]

Naturally the Regent was not satisfied with this performance of his Parlement. He had thought that the temporary subservience of the court would allow him to ram the declaration through, but he had been mistaken. Dubois, equally shaken, proposed that the declaration be registered by the *Grand Conseil*, another of the sovereign courts of Paris. For want of any better solution this advice was taken. On September 18, 1720, the declaration was sent to the *Grand Conseil* with a demand for rapid registration.

The declaration took the magistrates of the *Grand Conseil* completely by surprise. They had not been warned in advance for fear they would oppose the move. They were not used to registering edicts and did not know exactly what to do, but they did know that they did not want to register the declaration. Given courage by the example of the Parlement, they finally decided not to, but

[11] "Registres du conseil secret de Parlement de Paris," A.N., série X (1A) 8438, fols. 262–64, September 7, 1720; "Minutes du conseil secret de Parlement de Paris," A.N., série X (1B) 8901, item 22, September 7, 1720; Delisle, *Journal du Parlement*, A.N., série U 747, pp. 27–28; Dorsanne, *Journal de la Constitution "Unigenitus,"* II, 18; Villefore, *Anecdotes ou Mémoires secrètes*, III, 215; Marais, *Journal et Mémoires*, I, 425; Marsy (ed.), *Le Parlement à Pontoise*, 12.

instead to ask the Regent to take his edict back. Some even voted for a remonstrance.[12]

This defiance was too much. The Regent did not withdraw the declaration, nor did he permit a remonstrance. He came himself to the *Grand Conseil* on September 23 to herd his edict through personally. He brought the princes of the blood, the peers, and the marshals with him—twenty-six in all. Combined with the masters of Requests and councilors of state, they outnumbered the magistrates. Registration was assured even before the discussion began, although the Regent gave solemn assurance that he would not tamper with the voting. He did not have to. His picked troops did their part, and even the magistrates of the *Grand Conseil* fell into line. Only three votes were cast for a remonstrance. The declaration was registered and the next day was published in the streets of Paris.[13]

With this the religious quarrel seemed to be closed. The Regent and Dubois were greatly relieved. Their satisfaction, however, scarcely lasted beyond their day of triumph in the *Grand Conseil*. Both men were greatly shocked to find that they were alone in thinking that registration before the *Grand Conseil* was sufficient. So great was the reputation of the Parlement as a defender

[12] Marais, *Journal et Mémoires*, I, 434–37; Villefore, *Anecdotes ou Mémoires secrètes*, III, 216–17, 228–30, 242–44; Marsy, *Le Parlement à Pontoise*, 13–14; Dorsanne, *Journal de la Constitution "Unigenitus,"* II, 24–30.

[13] "Relation de ce qui s'est passé au Grand Conseil au sujet de la Déclaration du Roy donné le 4 aoust touchant la conciliation des Evesques du Royaume," A.N., AD +960; Delisle, *Journal du Parlement*, A.N., série U 747, pp. 32–33; Marais, *Journal et Mémoires*, I, 444–48; Barbier, *Journal historique et anecdotique*, I, 55–56; Dorsanne, *Journal de la Constitution "Unigenitus,"* II, 29–31; Villefore, *Anecdotes ou Mémoires secrètes*, III, 239–46; Saint-Simon, *Mémoires*, XXXVIII, 7–9.

of the Gallican liberties that the appellant bishops, led by Cardinal Noailles, refused to recognize the declaration unless it was registered by the Parlement. The problems of a recalcitrant clergy and a disobedient court became even more closely entwined. Discreet pressure on the cardinal had failed. Overt pressure on the Parlement would now be necessary.

The Regent and his minister planned their next series of moves carefully. Although the two did not really understand the power of moral force, they did understand that acceptance of the declaration of August 4 must be a voluntary act on the part of the Jansenist bishops and could not be coerced. Only a genuine acceptance could close the schism, if even that could. Moreover, the increasing irregularity of the Regent's actions, set against the background of Law's disaster, was gravely undermining confidence in his rule. Further violence against the accepted way of doing things would only bring diminishing returns. All this gave the cardinal and the Parlement a fairly strong bargaining position with the crown, if they could use it. The Regent, of course, was not unprotected. His ministers, particularly Dubois, were astute and strong. He had survived the first shock of the deflation of Law's system and was in control of the powers of government. His enemies were uncertain and divided.

The Regent began to put pressure on the Parlement. The judicial functions of the court came first. On September 23, just after the *Grand Conseil* registration, an order in council was published evoking from the Parlement to the more compliant *Grand Conseil* all cases, appeals, and civil actions arising from the implementation of the declaration.[14] Besides being a means of reducing magisterial incomes, this eliminated a whole range of cases from the Parlement's jurisdiction and reduced the scope of the Parlement's judicial politics. Although not immediately injurious, it posed an ultimately serious threat to the prestige and power of the court.

The nature of this threat was lost on no one. As early as September 28 negotiations between the Parlement and Cardinal Noailles were initiated. The cardinal, more stubborn than intelligent, was still holding his ground but looked more and more to the Parlement to give him a way out. And the magistrates, aware of the drift of royal policy, were eager to help him find that way. Neither the cardinal nor the magistrates fully realized what strengths they had; nor had they the nerve to hold out in any case. They caved in almost at once and began to look for a safe retreat. No sooner had the Regent and Dubois discovered this than they entered the conversations and pursued their quarry without mercy. The mere fact of discussion soon reduced the issue to how far and how fast the cardinal and court would retreat.

The channel of these negotiations was Father Guillaume Menguy, a noted Jansenist and an influential member of the *Grand' Chambre.* An honorable man, he had the confidence both of the First President and of the cardinal and the respect of the Regent. He tried first to get the cardinal to publish his acceptance of the declaration and take the pressure off the Parlement. At the same time he lobbied in the court for registration. This ground had already been covered by de Mesmes in early September, and both

[14] "Lettres patentes portant évocation et attribution au Grand Conseil de toutes les contestations nées et à naître au sujet de la Constitution 'Unigenitus,'" B.N., série F 23622 (347), September 23, 1720; Marais, *Journal et Mémoires,* I, 452–53.

of Menguy's attempts failed. He next met with Chancellor Aguesseau and drew up a set of modifications acceptable to both the cardinal and de Mesmes. The breach seemed almost healed when, toward the end of October, the Regent had the chancellor reject the modified declaration. This killed the negotiations, for the Regent's terms, now vastly increased, were unacceptable to both the cardinal and the Parlement.[15]

As soon as he learned of the conversations between Menguy, the cardinal, and de Mesmes, Dubois sensed victory. Attempting to keep the Parlement under pressure and to apply a spur to Father Menguy, the Regent and Dubois moved against the court. On October 7 the Regent created an extra-parlementary Interim Chamber in Paris. Composed of nine councilors of state and twenty-five masters of Requests—all royal officials—this new court was to hear the civil and criminal cases which would normally come before the Parlement.[16] Although not suppressed, the Parlement was stripped of all function. The new tribunal was to serve for only two months, but the intention was clear. The Regent did not necessarily consider the Parlement a permanent fixture of government.

[15] Dorsanne, *Journal de la Constitution "Unigenitus,"* II, 32–37. There are almost no sources for these semi-secret and highly important negotiations of Menguy with de Mesmes, Cardinal Noailles, and the Chancellor. Nevertheless, I have taken Dorsanne's word in the matter. Normally highly reliable, a canon of Notre Dame and a Jansenist friend of Menguy, Dorsanne was close to the actual negotiations. The other principals are silent, as far as I know. At any rate, in the absence of definite evidence to the contrary, this episode, so characteristic of the Regent's government and so plausible in the event, has been included.

[16] Règlement pour la Chambre des Vacations," B.N., série F 23622 (354), October 7, 1720; "Lettres Patentes du Roy en forme de commission portant éstablissement d'une Chambre des Vacations dans le couvent des Grands Augustins de Paris," B.N., série F 23622 (354), October, 1720.

Dubois, who was Cardinal Noailles' personal enemy, did not fail to notice the cardinal's repeated insistence that he could not publish his acceptance of the declaration until it was registered by the Parlement. Frantic to acquire a red hat before the Regent's drinking killed him, Dubois pressed the cardinal again and again. When the cardinal refused, Dubois turned to the Regent for support, advancing the theory that the court and the cardinal were in concord to try to force concessions. Outraged, the Regent resolved on further pressure. He would strike, or at least threaten to strike, a blow from which the Parlement might never recover.

The Interim Chamber in Paris had not been a success. Lawyers licensed to practice before the Parlement had refused to take cases to it, and others were reluctant to do so for fear they would never get their parlementary license. The Chamber had judged no cases. It had not substantially threatened the Parlement, but something more might. The Regent and Dubois began to drop hints that big things were in store for the Parlement. The court might be exiled farther away. Blois was prominently mentioned, but nothing was known for certain. The technique of the news leak was used to perfection.

Le Blanc, the Secretary of War, was the instrument of the leak. He told President Morceau, who informed President Hénault, who told Menguy.[17] Hénault and Menguy began by trying to line up support within the Parlement for a capitulation to the Regent which would block possible exile to Blois. On November 6 they went to see

[17] Dorsanne, *Journal de la Constitution "Unigenitus,"* II, 37; Charles Jean François Hénault, *Mémoires*, ed. François Rousseau (Paris, 1911), 291–92. Hénault gives a long and detailed account of his considerable part in the negotiations to stave off exile to Blois. This parallels the earlier attempts of Menguy and is also reported by Dorsanne.

President Chauvelin. Chauvelin felt himself unable to act. In a helpless tone he stated that he knew of the danger to the court and thought that everyone ought to meet this new exile firmly. He greatly bewailed the fact that the court had become tied to the political fortunes of Cardinal Noailles, for the Regent clearly believed that there was a compact between the Parlement and the prelate. Chauvelin then trailed off into aphorisms about magisterial virtue and courage in facing adversity.[18]

The next day the renewed negotiations began to bring results. Hénault and Menguy went to see de Mesmes. They asked him to go to Paris to see the Regent, and the First President agreed. He had previously been reluctant to do this, afraid that because of his ultramontane views he would be accused of surrender and lose the confidence of his court. But now crisis was in the air. The ultramontane magistrate had stood by his Parlement until it began to appear that there would no longer be any Parlement. De Mesmes and his negotiators were in no doubt that exile to Blois would be the preliminary step to complete suppression. The judicial functions of the court could only diminish with the Parlement far from its adjuncts, the police courts, its lawyers, and the support of the other sovereign courts of Paris. Add to this the inconvenience and expense of commuting to Blois for justice and appeals, and it was easy to see the Parlement heading for obscurity in a provincial backwater. Finally, the clients and lawyers who had hesitated to use the extra-parlementary Interim Chamber would be less reluctant to do so if it were clear that the Parlement's replacement was to be permanent.

[18] Dorsanne, *Journal de la Constitution "Unigenitus,"* II, 38.

Pressure on Cardinal Noailles paralleled that on the Parlement. On November 8 the cardinal received a note from Chancellor Aguesseau telling him that unless he accepted the declaration of August 4 the Parlement would be destroyed. That same afternoon the Regent called the cardinal to the Palais Royal and told him the same thing. The cardinal would concede only to meeting with the First President that evening to work something out. The Regent grudgingly agreed.[19]

Working the other side of the street, the Regent conferred with de Mesmes on the tenth. The First President was ordered to persuade Cardinal Noailles to publish his acceptance of the declaration. The unhappy magistrate had been trying to do this for nearly two months but said that he would try again. However, the stubborn cardinal would not budge. This bad news reached the Regent during a meeting of the Council of Regency. All hope for a negotiated peace seemed to have vanished. If de Mesmes could not move the cardinal, who could? Bitter and baffled, the Regent saw no alternative to going through with the exile to Blois. The term would open there on December 12. *Lettres de cachet* were ordered for all magistrates, informing them of the decision.[20]

This decision broke up the solidarity of the ministry. Chancellor Aguesseau refused to seal the order and informed the Regent that he was going to resign. Marshal Villars, the leading soldier of France, joined in the efforts to save the court. Continuous, frantic negotiations were begun at once among the Regent, Villars, the cardinal, the

<hr />

[19] *Ibid.*, II, 39–41; Hénault, *Mémoires*, 306.

[20] Delisle, *Journal du Parlement*, A.N., série U 747, p. 41; Dorsanne, *Journal de la Constitution "Unigenitus,"* II, 40; Barbier, *Journal historique et anecdotique*, I, 58; Marais, *Journal et Mémoires*, I, 477–78; Hénault, *Mémoires*, 307–308; Villars, *Mémoires*, IV, 145.

chancellor, and Menguy and Hénault. Villars and Advocate-General Lamoignon went to the cardinal, informed him of the impending exile, and convinced him to accept the declaration. Villars reported at once to de Mesmes and the Regent. Two months of increasing pressure had finally moved Cardinal Noailles. De Mesmes was lobbying for registration among his magistrates. Assisted by Menguy, he pointed out the folly of further resistance and began to line up the councilors for registration. This time he convinced nearly everyone.[21]

On November 14 the bargain was sealed. Villars, having seen Dubois, found him adamant, willing to accept total victory but nothing less. He took this to de Mesmes, whom he found discussing the surrender with Menguy, the cardinal, and Chancellor Aguesseau. The cardinal renewed his acceptance of the declaration, which de Mesmes assured him the court would register.[22]

The next morning the cardinal told the Regent that he would publish his acceptance and asked that the declaration be sent back to the Parlement. With the cardinal's acceptance in his pocket, the Regent began to patch things up with his Parlement. He issued letters patent transferring cases concerning the declaration from the *Grand Conseil* back to the Parlement.[23] He told de Mesmes that the transfer to Blois was cancelled. The

[21] Delisle, *Journal du Parlement*, A.N., série U 747, p. 42; Villars, *Mémoires,* IV 145–49; Dorsanne, *Journal de la Constitution "Unigenitus,"* II, 41–43; Barbier, *Journal historique et anecdotique,* I, 59.

[22] Delisle, *Journal du Parlement*, A.N., série U 747, p. 43; Dorsanne, *Journal de la Constitution "Unigenitus,"* II, 44; Hénault, *Mémoires,* 310–11; Villars, *Mémoires,* IV, 148.

[23] "Lettres Patentes portant évocation et attribution au Parlement de Paris séant à Pontoise de toutes les contestations nées et à naître au sujet de Constitution 'Unigenitus,'" B.N., série F 23622 (380), November 25, 1720.

Parlement would get the declaration back, and he hoped that it would be registered without delay.[24]

On December 2 the Parlement met to reconsider the declaration. De Mesmes introduced it with a short speech written by Menguy. The First President spoke of the modifications made in the 1714 registration of *Unigenitus,* the evils of religious schism, and the disasters that had befallen the Parlement in the conduct of its public duty. But now there must be registration. This moderate speech won general applause.[25]

Again commissioners were named, and de Mesmes took the precaution of putting himself and Menguy on the commission. Although the Jansenist Father Pucelle spoke against the declaration, he was opposed by Menguy, which made a considerable impression on the others. To reinforce this de Mesmes reminded the magistrates that the condition for discussing the declaration at all was its registration. Otherwise, the Parlement would find itself in Blois. This carried the barricades, and the commissioners, handpicked by de Mesmes, reported favorably on the declaration after a single day of discussion. On September 4 the entire court considered the declaration and the report of the commissioners. Only six dissenting votes were heard, and the Declaration was registered "conforming to the rules of the Church and to the maxims of the Kingdom on the authority of the Church, to the

[24] Delisle, *Journal du Parlement,* A.N., série U 747, p. 43; Villars, *Mémoires,* IV, 150; Dorsanne, *Journal de la Constitution "Unigenitus,"* II, 45; Marais, *Journal et Mémoires,* II, 14–15.

[25] "Registres du conseil secret de Parlement de Paris," A.N., série X (1A) 8438 fols. 270–75, December 2, 1720; "Minutes du conseil secret de Parlement de Paris," A.N., série X (1B) 8901, item 1, December 2, 1720; Marais, *Journal et Mémoires,* II, 3; Dorsanne, *Journal de la Constitution "Unigenitus,"* II, 49–50, Hénault, *Mémoires,* 330–33, for text of the speech. Delisle, *Journal du Parlement,* A.N., série U 747, p. 50.

power and jurisdiction of the bishops, to the acceptance of bulls of the Popes, and to the appeals to a future council, which maxims and rules remain in their former state. . . ." Although this rider might easily be viewed as at variance with the body of the edict, particularly concerning future councils and maxims of the Church, no one was really concerned. Dubois and the Regent had all they felt they could, or should, ask for. Not that they feared the Parlement; exile had proved that they did not. But the crown might not always find itself on the side of Rome, and a little ambiguity would be good insurance. If the declaration itself did not satisfy Clement, he could be threatened with further modifications. Politics made strange turns. One never knew. In any case, the immediate crisis was over. Rome and Dubois were satisfied, and the Parlement could return to Paris.[26]

The exile to Pontoise was sort of "historic," as municipal chambers of commerce are wont to use the word. It was the last royal victory over the Parlement in a real showdown. Thereafter, in 1749, 1753, 1771–74, and 1788, exile of the court would end in concessions by the ministers. In 1720 it did not. The Regent and Dubois got exactly what they wanted, and the Parlement was forced to concede every point.

This was mostly the result of a strong and determined government. Normally considered weak and inefficient, the Regency ministries after the spring of 1718 were actually strong and filled with competent men. Saint-Simon's *polysynodie* has cast a pall over the Regency and

[26] "Registres du conseil secret de Parlement de Paris," A.N., série X (1A) 8438, fols. 279–80, December 4, 1720, and fols. 292–97, December 17, 1720; "Minutes du conseil secret de Parlement de Paris," A.N., série X (1B) 8901, item 6, December 4, 1720; December 17, 1720; Delisle, *Journal du Parlement*, A.N., série U 747, pp. 50–53.

made it appear as though government and administration were in the hands of children and fools. Nothing could be farther from the truth. The single best clue to this is the large number of experimental policies carried out by the Regent. In foreign policy he switched from a Spanish alliance to one with the ancient enemy, England, and in 1719 fought a successful war against Spain. In the finances the system of John Law was introduced and liquidated after a disastrous collapse. With regard to religion, the Regent changed from a Gallican to an ultramontane policy with almost no real trouble. Concerning the Parlement, he was able to use the court as an agent of government in religion and crush it when it opposed him. He changed his ministers and policies often. The Regent was in control of his government and of France.

Part of the success against the Parlement in 1720 can be traced to the political capacities of Father Dubois. With regard to the Parlement Dubois had one simple objective. He was not trying to accomplish some vague mission of forcing the court to recognize the primacy of royal power. Dubois wanted the declaration of August 4 registered—nothing more, nothing vague, nothing impossible. Dubois and his master merely wanted obedience on a single issue. It was possible, though not easy, to obtain this. Later ministeries would find more ambitious projects harder to fulfill.

Even this limited project of registering the declaration did not produce all the benefits hoped for, although Dubois and the Regent probably got everything they could reasonably expect. The religious schism was not really healed. Jansenism flared up again in the 1730's over the *convulsionaires,* and the Parlement defended the dissidents. Cardinal Noailles proved to be only a very lukewarm ultramontane. The Gallicans still muttered in the background, and the satirical Jansenist newspaper, *Nouvelles Ecclésiastiques,* was widely read and quoted. But the breach with Rome was closed.

For many of the participants the exile to Pontoise concluded happily. The ultramontane First President de Mesmes had shown great firmness and loyalty to his court in the crisis and considerable diplomatic ability in bringing the exile to an end. As a result of this, the distrust previously shown him by his Gallican colleagues vanished, and he now had the complete confidence and loyalty of the Parlement. Father Menguy vastly increased his reputation for wisdom and moderation, and his stature within the Parlement was immense. The Regent finally reduced the Parlement to its proper state of obedience and had no more trouble with it for the rest of his life. In the three years of the Regency which remained, the Parlement conducted its politics as the Regent had hoped it would in 1715. And in 1722, some months before his death, Dubois became a cardinal.

CHAPTER X

Epilogue:
The End of the Regency
and Beyond

THE ROAD HOME from Pontoise was bedecked with outward rejoicing. The magistrates received the congratula-
lations of the corps of lawyers licensed to practice before
them and the good wishes of the sister sovereign courts
of Paris. The Regent and his ministers sent conciliatory
messages. The satisfaction of the people of Paris was
evident. All seemed well, with the right and traditional
relationships between crown and court restored. Christ-
mas and the attendant celebrations added to the general
satisfaction surrounding the end of a crisis. And yet the
lawyer Marais wrote for everyone when he noted, "God,
give us a new year better than the last." [1]

This return of the prodigal was, in reality, a small
event. For the first time since the Regency began, the
Parlement left the center of the political stage. The real
crisis was not with the Parlement but elsewhere. Prices
of basic items—bread, wine, cheese, firewood—were twice
as high in December, 1720, as they had been three years
ago, and real wages had dropped by 30 per cent.[2] Unem-

[1] Marais, *Journal et Mémoires*, II, 40.
[2] See the superb pair of articles by Earl Hamilton, "Prices and
Wages at Paris under John Law's System," *Quarterly Journal of Eco-*

ployment, destitution, and starvation were more common than at any time since the War of the Spanish Succession. Law's paper was worthless. Shopkeepers refused it; vendors lit fires with it. Men who had thought themselves wealthy were on the rates. In the uncertain economic climate trade stagnated and credit dried up. Specie was hoarded, and people tried barter or paper. Taxes in coin were uncollectable; only paper was offered.

While the wealthy were hurt, the poor suffered horribly from a vicious price and wage squeeze. Even craftsmen who were employed or owned their own shops felt the bite of depression. But the servants or journeymen, the migrants from the countryside, the landless laborers, the urban beggars—these were the wretched victims of Law's system. The concentrated charity of the Church could hardly sustain them, and many starved in the dank, gray alleys of the Faubourg du Temple or Saint-Antoine. Petty crime rose and increased again, and Cartouche became a popular hero. The periodic periods of starvation inevitable in Old Regime France had come again. The face of God was averted from His people. In such times what did the starving wretches or even the bourgeois care for the Gallican liberties, the constitutionalism of the Parlement, or the debt of the crown? Against the warp of want, the issues of politics and the Parlement disappeared. The problems of society belonged to the Regent and his advisors, and solutions must come from the crown.

The very magnitude of Law's disaster and the rapid recovery during the end of the Regency and under Cardinal

nomics, LI (1936–37), and "Prices and Wages in Southern France under John Law's System," *Economic Journal, Economic History Supplement* (February, 1937).

Fleury were factors in the Parlement's political retreat. For what could the magistrates do? Only the Regent could ameliorate the collapse of Law's system. From him alone could come coin for paper or rebates and annulment of taxes. Only the crown could import grain and drive prices down again. Politics, economics, and war demanded the powers and prerogatives of the crown. The Parlement could not perform the monarch's executive functions.

The return from Pontoise, then, implied an agreement in which the magistrates would leave the direction of policy to the Regent. Both the events of the time and the Parlement's submission tended toward this end. Once in Paris the magistrates displayed the utmost discretion on issues for which they had previously risked all. The liquidation of John Law's system passed without a word. No mention was made of the plight of the poor who were made beggars by the collapse of the notes and were now on the streets. The fathers of families, whose case had been pleaded so tearfully in the remonstrance of March, 1720, were now forgotten. The Gallican clergy, who had placed their forlorn hopes in the Parlement, were abandoned to the declaration of August. From 1720 until the end of the Regency, in fact until the religious crisis of 1730, the Parlement of Paris would play only a minor role in the affairs of state. In sharp contrast to the first five years of the Regency and the 1750's, the involvement of the Parlement would be peripheral. The men and the causes which the Parlement had sustained seemed lost and forgotten.

After Pontoise the Parlement sank into a fairly prolonged political lethargy, and justice replaced politics as the function of magistrates. Nearly eighteen months passed before they commented on any political issue at all. Although the Parlement possessed all the legal weapons and rights in politics that it had previously, the magistrates were deterred by the Regent's obvious displeasure. But in May, 1722, the court roused itself to protest the Regent's taxes. Having tried everything else, the Regent turned to taxation to raise money and balance his budget. In March he drew up an order in council reimposing several taxes he had earlier suppressed and adding a tax on the administration of justice.[3] It was a measure of the strain on the treasury imposed by the recovery from Law that the Regent turned to taxes which he himself felt undesirable and had once suppressed.

The Parlement decided to consider the issue of new taxes, even though the order in council had not been sent to it. Long discussion revealed that the magistrates were completely opposed to the new taxes. Sixty-seven voted for a remonstrance, the rest for further consideration of the matter.[4] When discussion was resumed ten days later, the magistrates had talked themselves into a remonstrance.[5] Appalled by the unaccustomed activity

[3] Marais, *Journal et Mémoires,* II, 269; "Déclaration du Roy portant rétablissement de plusiers droits," B.N., série F 23622 (608), May 15, 1722.

[4] Marais, *Journal et Mémoires,* II, 280; "Registres du conseil secret de Parlement de Paris, A.N., série X (1A) 8440, fols. 196–97, April 27, 1722; "Minutes du conseil secret de Parlement de Paris," A.N., série X (1B) 8902, item 47, April 27, 1722.

[5] "Registres du conseil secret de Parlement de Paris," A.N., série X (1A) 8440, fols. 262–63, May 7, 1722; "Minutes du conseil secret de Parlement de Paris," A.N., série X (1B) 8903, item 13, May 7, 1722; Villars, *Mémoires,* IV, 225–26; Flammermont (ed.), *Les Remontrances,* I, 148; Barbier, *Journal historique et anecdotique,* I, 144; Buvat, *Journal de la Régence,* II, 383–84; "Registres du conseil secret de Parlement de Paris," A.N., série X (1A) 8440, fols. 289–90, May 16, 1722; "Minutes du

of the Parlement, the Regent at first forbade one. But middle age had accentuated his ruling qualities, the first of which was amiability, and, sensing no danger from the remonstrance and not wishing to further disgrace the magistrates, he reversed himself and permitted the protest.

Fortunate at having been allowed to complain at all, the magistrates produced a sober, moderate remonstrance. It began with the assertion that the wealth of the people was the real grandeur of the King. Now a great number of burdensome taxes were being re-established. The magistrates did not doubt that this was necessary, but the King ought not to forget the unfavorable aspects of heavy taxation. These particular duties were laid on common articles—meat, drink, fodder, cloth—all, in fact, except grain and wood. Did the King find himself in such a state that he must levy imposts on the poor and collect taxes that thirty years of war had scarcely accustomed France to? There were taxes placed on justice, too, which would render it much more accessible to the rich than to the poor. This was unjust and disturbed the magistrates greatly. The short remonstrance closed with the comment that the Parlement relied on the good will of the King and the Regent and did not wish to diminish royal authority. The court only hoped to do its duty toward the crown and God.[6] Unimpressed, the Regent merely replied that the edict was to be registered "at the very express command of the King." [7] The crown needed the money.

---

conseil secret de Parlement de Paris," A.N., série X (1B) 8903, item 43, May 16, 1722.

[6] Text is in Flammermont (ed.), Les Remontrances, I, 148–52.

[7] Ibid., I, 153; Marais, Journal et Mémoires, II, 290; Buvat, Journal de la Régence, II, 394; "Registres du conseil secret de Parlement de Paris," A.N., série X (1A) 8440, fols. 318–20, May 20, 1722; "Minutes

But these new taxes still did not satisfy the Regent's need for cash, which could probably never be satisfied. A classic victim of Parkinson's Second Law, the crown was absolutely unable to find revenues to meet its expenses. Its income could never be adequate. The summer was spent, therefore, looking for new fiscal expedients, and one was found. This time the rich were to be taxed. In August, 1722, two edicts were sent to the Parlement. The first abolished the right of hereditary succession of offices, the right of an office owner to pass his post on to an heir, and re-established the Paulette, an annual tax on the purchase price of the office. The magistrates of the Parlement, however, were specifically exempted from the new tax.[8] The second edict re-established many municipal offices which the Regent had earlier suppressed. These were created because the necessity to "re-imburse the capital of the debts of the state obliges us to look for the most convenient means to bring it about. It appears to us the most sure and least onerous expedient to be the re-establishment of many different offices suppressed since our advent to the Crown. . . ."[9] These offices were to be sold for the benefit of the treasury to enterprising bourgeois who wanted to move up in the world. In both cases the edicts were designed to tap the resources of those wealthy and privileged enough to escape ordinary forms of taxation.

---

du conseil secret de Parlement de Paris," A.N., série X (1B) 8903, item 62, May 20, 1722.

[8] "Déclaration du Roy portant révocation de la survivance attribué par l'édit du mois de Décembre 1709 et rétablissement du droit annuel des offices et charges," B.N., série F 23622 (640), August 9, 1722; Marais, *Journal et Mémoires,* II, 344; Buvat, *Journal de la Régence,* II, 416.

[9] "Edit du Roy pour création et rétablissement des officiers municipaux et autres," B.N., série F 23622 (633), August, 1722.

On August 26 the two edicts were read to the Parlement. They created an uproar. The magistrates felt personally threatened and unanimously voted to remonstrate.[10] This protest was somewhat stronger than the last, though still plaintive in tone. In May the King had established new taxes. At that time the Parlement believed that the levies would be of short duration, but now taxes were being increased again, and in a most objectionable manner. Louis XIV, desperately short of money because of his wars, had created and sold many offices which had no function at all and which the privileged bought. It was difficult for the crown to imagine the enormous human and financial cost to the people of even the smallest office. France needed fewer of them, not more. Superfluous offices should never have been created in the first place and should not be re-established.

The second part of the remonstrance concerned the elimination of hereditary succession. This form of reversion was established to give offices stability, but now a levy was proposed which would undermine this and tax the King's most useful subjects. Judicial and administrative officials might lose their offices from such a tax. The most worthy men would no longer wish to become magistrates. Even the King would lose. Sale of offices had succeeded previously because people had regarded them as fixed property which could be inherited. Who could benefit from breaking this contract?[11] The Regent concluded that the crown could and ordered the Parle-

[10] "Registres du conseil secret de Parlement de Paris," A.N., série X (1A) 8441, fols. 41–45, August 26, 1722; "Minutes du conseil secret de Parlement de Paris," A.N., série X (1B) 8903, items 49–51, August 26, 1722; Flammermont (ed.), Les Remontrances, I, 153.

[11] Text is in Flammermont (ed.), Les Remontrances, I, 154–61.

ment to register the two edicts immediately. The apprehensive magistrates did so.[12]

This kind of political action was clearly what the Regent had in mind when he granted the Parlement the remonstrance in 1715. He had thought of the magistrates giving advice and retiring from the scene if that advice were ignored. He had thought of the Parlement as a political ally, who would register royal edicts cheerfully and without public complaint. He had anticipated remonstrances, but had not thought the magistrates capable of a full vendetta. He had hoped that the Parlement would be a cooperating part of the government and not an independent corporation with a policy of its own. For seven years he battled with his Parlement with varying success, until, near the end of his life in 1722, he obtained what he had sought since 1715.

For the Parlement and its magistrates the Regency opened in triumph and ended in despair. For seven years the Parlement fought the Regent and lost. In the short view one sees nothing but wreckage. With the finances the magistrates had had no success, and Law's system had run its course. The opposition of the Parlement had meant almost nothing. It was the same with the Gallican liberties. Dubois and the Regent pushed their compromise through and forced the magistrates to accede to it. The Parlement's constitutional pretensions were crushed

[12] *Ibid.*, I, 161; "Registres du conseil secret de Parlement de Paris," A.N., série X (1A) 8441, fols. 95–99, September 3, 1722; "Minutes du conseil secret de Parlement de Paris," A.N., série X (1B) 8903, items 12–13, September 3, 1722; Buvat, *Journal de la Régence*, II, 415–16; "Registres du conseil secret de Parlement de Paris," A.N., série X (1A) 8841, fols. 115–19, September 5, 1722; "Minutes du conseil secret de Parlement de Paris," A.N., série X (1B) 8903, items 23–25, September 5, 1722.

in the *lit de justice* of 1718. Nothing seemed changed from the reign of the Sun King.

But the short view is not the only view. The Parlement had gained increased institutional powers during the Regency. The right of remonstrance had been returned, and with it all the unmeasured possibilities of appealing directly to the people. The Regent implicitly recognized the necessity of the Parlement's registration of edicts, and the court was treated as a political force and accorded the respect which accompanies power. During the Regency the magistrates made that power felt only sporadically; perhaps later they would do better.

In any case the magistrates would try. During the religious conflicts over Jansenism of the 1730's they fought Cardinal Fleury to the end. But they lost. From 1749 to 1751, however, the Parlement played a large role in defeating Machault's proposals for a tax on the privileged. In 1762 the Parlement suppressed the Jesuits, and in 1787–88 forced the calling of the Estates-General. Aided by a weak King and favorable public opinion, the Parlement was able to force its views on the crown. The political powers acquired and exercised during the Regency were quite sufficient for a parlementary victory.

The politics of the Regency, and the views of the magistrates of the Regency Parlement, are a prototype of what was to come during the rest of the Old Regime. The magistrates never relinquished their views about the right and fundamental laws of France and the place of their court in the French constitutions. Nor did the Parlement's obsession with the financial rights of the privileged ever wane. The court did not end its vendetta against the Jesuits until the Society had been hounded out of France. The Parlement's Regency politics, both views and strategy, would be played over and over during the rest of the eighteenth century, eventually with fatal success. During the Regency the days and ways of the Sun King were not so far off. But the magistrates had begun to pursue their vision of the Parlement of Paris as the nation assembled.

BIBLIOGRAPHY

BIBLIOGRAPHIES AND GUIDES

Antoine, Michel, and others. *Guide des recherches dans les fonds judiciaires de l'ancien régime.* Paris, 1958.

Antoine, Michel. *Les fonds du conseil d'Etat du Roi aux archives nationales.* Paris, 1955.

Isnard, A., and others (eds.). *Catalogue général des livres imprimés de la Bibliothèque Nationale: Actes Royaux.* Paris, 1910–57.

Stein, Henri. *Répertoire numérique des Archives du Parlement de Paris.* Paris, 1889.

MANUSCRIPT SOURCES

Archives Nationales

Section Judiciaire: Série U, Mélanges Judiciaires.
   Collection Delisle
      November, 1715–June, 1716—No. 358.
      July, 1716–September, 1716—No. 359.
      November, 1716–October, 1717—No. 360.
      November, 1717–October, 1718—No. 361.
      November, 1718–October, 1719—No. 362.
      November, 1719–July, 1720—No. 363.
      November, 1720–October, 1721—No. 364.
      November, 1721–October, 1722—No. 365.
      November, 1722–October, 1723—No. 366.
   Journal du Parlement par Delisle, 1718—No. 416.

*Premières minutes des séances du conseil secret
rédigées par le greffier Gilbert,* 1718–22—Nos. 420–21.

*Lits de justice et Remonstrances du Parlement, Edits et
Déclarations du Roy, par Delisle,* 1714–25—No. 429.

Delisle, Jean-Gilbert. *Journal du Parlement séant à Pontoise
depuis 21 Juillet 1720 jusqu'à 11 Novembre*—Nos. 747–48.

Section Judiciaire: Série X, Archives du Parlement de Paris.

Registres civils; X (1A)

    Conseil—Nos. 3316–3413.

    Conseil secret—Nos. 8432–41.

    Lettres Patentes—Nos. 8714–27.

    Conclusions des procureurs-généraux—Nos. 8973–81.

    Saisies réeles—No. 9122.

Minutes civiles; X (1B)

    Conseil—Nos. 3173–3257.

    Conseil secret—Nos. 8897–8903.

    Lettres Patentes—Nos. 9011–16.

    Procès–verbaux des Comissaires—Nos. 9430–31.

Bibliothèque Nationale

Manuscrits Français.

Procès–verbaux du conseil de Régence, 1715–23—Nos.
23663–73.

Mémoires manuscrits du Torcy.

    1715–16—No. 10670.

    1717—No. 10671.

    1718—No. 10672.

Mémoire du duc de Noailles sur les finances, June 19–26,
1717—No. 11152.

Clairambault, Count of. "Relation de la séance au Parlement du 2 septembre 1715."—No. 719, fols. 529–44.

PRINTED PRIMARY SOURCES

Collections of Official Documents

Actes Royaux. *Bibliothèque Nationale.*

August, 1715–December, 1718–F 23621 (121–1024).

January, 1719–July, 1723–F 23622 (1–812).

Recueils des arrêts du Conseil d'Etat. *Bibliothèque Nationale.*
August, 1715–December, 1716–F 23649 (402–850).

January, 1717–December, 1718–F 23650 (1–847).

January, 1719–December, 1720–F 23651 (1–1332).

January, 1721–December, 1722–F 23652 (1–1235).

January–March, 1723–F 23653 (1–169).

Recueils des arrêts du Parlement de Paris. *Bibliothèque Nationale.* 1714–24–F 23672 (1–464).

Censures et Conclusions de la sacrée Faculté de Théologie de Paris touchant la souveraineté des Rois, la fidélité que leurs doivent leurs Sujets, la sûreté de leurs Personnes, et la tranquillité de l'Etat. Paris, 1720.

Dufey, P. J. S. *Histoire, actes et remontrances des Parlemens de France.* . . . 2 vols. Paris, 1826.

Flammermont, Jules (ed.). *Remontrances du Parlement de Paris au XVIIIe siècle.* 3 vols. Paris, 1888–98.

Funck-Brentano, Frantz. *Les Lettres de cachet à Paris, étude, suivie d'une liste des prisonniers de la Bastille, 1659–1789.* Paris, 1903.

Isambert, François André, and others (eds.). *Recueil général des anciennes lois françaises depuis l'an 420 jusqu'à la révolution de 1789.* 29 vols. Paris, 1821–33.

Laurière, Eusèbe J. de. *Recueil d'édits et d'ordonnances royaux sur le fait de la justice et autres matières les plus importantes.* 2 vols. Paris, 1720.

Le Moy, A. *Remontrances du Parlement de Bretagne au XVIIIe siècle.* Angers, 1909.

Mention, Léon (ed.). *Documents relatifs aux rapports du clergé avec la Royauté de 1705 à 1789.* 2 vols. Paris, 1893–1903.

Memoirs and Journals

Aguesseau, Henri François d'. *Lettres inédites,* ed. D. B. Rives. Paris, 1823.

——. *Oeuvres complètes du Chancelier d'Aguesseau,* ed. Jean Marie Pardessus. 16 vols. Paris, 1819.

Aligre, Etienne d'. "Relation de ce qui se passa au Parlement de Paris à la mort de Louis XIV," *Revue Rétrospective,* 2e série, VI (1836).

Argenson, René Louis de Voyer, Marquis of. *Journal et Mémoires,* ed. E. J. B. Rathéry. 9 vols. Paris, 1859–67.

Barbier, E. J. F. *Journal historique et anecdotique du règne de Louis XV, 1718–1763,* ed. A. de la Villegille. 4 vols. Paris, 1847–56.

Barthelémy, Edouard de (ed.). *Les Correspondants de la Marquise de Balleroy, 1706–1725.* 2 vols. Paris, 1883.

——. *Gazette de la Régence.* Paris, 1887.

Boislisle, A. de (ed.). "Projet de discours pour le lit de justice du 2 septembre 1715," *Annuaire-Bulletin de la Société de l'histoire de France* (1880), 125–28.

Brunet, M. G. (ed.). *Correspondance complète de Madame, Duchesse d'Orléans.* 2 vols. Paris, 1891.

Buvat, Jean. *Journal de la Régence,* ed. B. Campardon. 2 vols. Paris, 1865.

Croÿ, Emmanuel, Duke of. *Journal inédit du Duc de Croÿ, 1718–1784,* eds. Grouchy and P. Cottin. 2 vols. Paris, 1906–1907.

Dangeau, Philippe de Courcillon, Marquis of. *Journal,* eds. Eudore Soulié and Louis Etienne Dussieux. 19 vols. Paris, 1854–60.

Dorsanne, A. *Journal contenant tout ce qui s'est passé à Rome et en France dans l'affaire de la Constitution "Unigenitus."* 2 vols. Paris, 1753.

Drumont, Edouard (ed.), *La Mort de Louis XIV: Journal des Anthoine publié pour le premier fois.* Paris, 1880.

Duclos, Charles. *Mémoires secrètes sur le règne de Louis XIV, la Régence et le règne de Louis XV.* 2 vols. Paris, 1808.

Forbonnais, François Véron de. *Recherches et considérations sur les finances de France depuis l'année 1559 jusqu'à l'année 1721.* 2 vols. Basle, 1758.

Gazette de France. December, 1716–23.

Hénault, Charles Jean François. *Mémoires,* ed. François Rousseau. Paris, 1911.

Joly, Claude. *Recueil des Maximes Véritables et Importantes pour l'Instruction du Roy contre la Pernicieuse politique du Cardinal Mazarin, Sur-Intendant de l'Education de Sa Majesté.* Paris, 1652, 1663.

Lafitau, Pierre. *Histoire de la Constitution "Unigenitus."* 2 vols. Avignon, 1737.

Lamoignon, Guillaume de. "Journal historique de Guillaume de Lamoignon avocat-général du Parlement de Paris, 1713–1718," ed. Henri Courteault, *Annuaire-Bulletin de la Société de l'histoire de France,* XLVII (1910), 238–95.

Law, John. *The Present State of the French revenues and trade, and of the controversy betwixt the Parliament of Paris and Mr. Law. . . .* London, 1720.

Le Bret, Cardin. *Traité de la Souveraineté du Roy, de son Domaine et de sa Couronne.* Paris, 1632.

Marais, Mathieu. *Journal et Mémoires sur la Régence et le règne de Louis XV,* ed. A. M. de Lescure. 4 vols. Paris, 1863–68.

Marsy, Arthur de (ed.). *Le Parlement à Pontoise en 1720: Journal rédigé par un cordelier du couvent de cette ville.* Paris, 1863.

Narbonne, Pierre. *Journal des règnes de Louis XIV et Louis XV de l'année 1701 à l'année 1744,* ed. J. A. Roi. Versailles, 1866.

Poissens, Chevalier de. *Mémoires de la Régence.* 3 vols. The Hague, 1729.

Raunié, Emile (ed.). *Chansonnier historique du XVIIIe siècle.* 10 vols. Paris, 1879–84.

Richelieu, Louis Armand, Duke of. *Mémoires authentiques du Maréchal de Richelieu,* ed. A. de Boislisle.

Saint-Simon, Louis de Rouvroy, Duke of. *Mémoires,* ed. A. de Boislisle. 41 vols. Paris, 1879–1928.

———. *Ecrits inédits de Saint-Simon,* ed. M. P. Faugère. 8 vols. Paris, 1881–93.

Seyssel, Claude de. *La Monarchie de France,* ed. Jacques Poujol. Paris, 1961. Originally presented to Francis I in 1515.

Soanen, Jean. *La vie et les lettres de Messire Jean Soanen, Evêque de Senez.* 2 vols. Cologne, 1750.

Les Tocsins avec les écrits et les arrêts publiés contre des libelles violentes et séditieux, avec un recueil des mandements et autres pièces qui ont rapport aux écrits précédents. Paris, 1716.

Villars, Claude Louis Hector, Marshal. *Mémoires,* ed. Marquis de Vogüe. 6 vols. Paris, 1884–1904.

Villefore de Bourgoin. *Anecdotes ou mèmoires secrètes sur la Constitution "Unigenitus."* 3 vols. Utrecht, 1734.

Voltaire. *Histoire du Parlement de Paris.* N.p., 1769.

SECONDARY SOURCES

Balteau, Barroux, Prévost, and others. *Dictionnaire de Biographie Française.* 9 vols. Paris, 1933–61.

Basieux, L. *Théorie des libertés gallicanes du Parlement de Paris au XVIIIe siècle.* Paris, 1906.

Baudrillart, Alfred. *Philippe V et la Cour de France.* 5 vols. Paris, 1890–1901.

Becker, Carl. *The Heavenly City of the Eighteenth Century Philosophers.* New Haven, 1959.

Bickart, Roger. *Les parlements et la notion de souveraineté nationale au XVIIIe siècle.* Paris, 1932.

Bluche, J. P. *L'Origine des magistrats du Parlement de Paris au XVIIIe siècle.* Paris, 1956. Volumes IV and V of *Mémoires de Fédération des sociétés historiques et archéologiques de Paris et de l'Ile de France.* Paris, 1949—.

Boulanger, Jacques. *The Seventeenth Century in France.* Capricorn edition, New York, 1963.

Cahen, Léon. *Les Querelles religieuses et parlementaires sous Louis XV.* Paris, 1913.

Carreyre, J. *Le Jansénisme durant la Régence.* 2 vols. Louvain, 1929–33.

Clamageran, J. J. *Histoire de l'impôt en France.* 3 vols. Paris, 1876.

Deteix, Genevieve. *Les arrêts de règlement du Parlement de Paris.* Paris, 1930.

Doolin, Paul. *The Fronde.* Cambridge, Mass., 1935.

Ford, Franklin. *Robe and Sword.* Cambridge, Mass, 1953.

Giesey, Ralph. *Juristic Basis of Dynastic Right.* Philadelphia, 1963.

Glasson, Etienne. *Le Parlement de Paris: Son role politique depuis le règne de Charles VII jusqu'à la révolution.* 2 vols. Paris, 1901.

Gooch, G .P. *Louis XV: The Monarchy in Decline.* London, 1956.

Hamilton, Earl. "Origin and Growth of the National Debt in Western Europe," *American Economic Review, Proceedings,* XXXVII (May, 1947), 118–40.

————. "Prices and Wages at Paris under John Law's System," *Quarterly Journal of Economics,* LI (1936–37), 42–70.

————. "Prices and Wages in Southern France under John Law's System," *Economic History, Economic Journal Supplement,* III (February, 1937), 441–61.

Kaplow, Jeffrey. *Elbeuf during the Revolutionary Period.* Baltimore, 1964.

Lacombe, Bernard. *La résistance janséniste et parlementaire au temps de Louis XV.* Paris, 1948.

Langlois, A. "Ancêtres de parlementaires parisiens," *Bulletin de la Société de l'Histoire de Paris et de l'Ile-de-France,* LIII (1926), 61–63.

Lecastre, Léon. "Le procès du Duc de la Force en 1721," *Revue des Questions Historiques,* CIII (October, 1925), 322–60.

Leclercq, Don H. *Histoire de la Régence.* 3 vols. Paris, 1922.

Lemaire, André. *Les lois fondamentales de la monarchie*

française d'après les théoriciens de l'ancien régime. Paris, 1907.

Lemontey, P. E. *Histoire de la Régence et de la minorité de Louis XV.* 2 vols. Paris, 1832.

Le Moy, A. *Le Parlement de Bretagne et le Pouvoir Royal au XVIIIe siècle.* Angers, 1909.

Lewis, W. H. *Louis XIV: An Informal Portrait.* New York, 1959.

Major, J. R. *Representative Institutions in Renaissance France, 1421–1559.* Madison, Wis., 1960.

Marion, Marcel. *Dictionnaire des institutions de la France aux XVIIe et XVIIIe siècles.* Paris, 1923.

——. *Histoire financière de la France depuis 1715.* 6 vols. Paris, 1914–31.

Martin, V. *Le Gallicanisme politique et le Clergé de France.* Paris, 1929.

Mason, Lester B. *The French Constitution and the Social Question in the Old Regime, 1700–1789.* Bonn, 1954.

Matthews, George T. *The Royal General Farms in Eighteenth Century France.* New York, 1958.

Moret, Ernest. *Quinze Ans du régne de Louis XIV.* 3 vols. Paris, 1859.

Mousnier, R., and Hartung, F. "Quelques problèmes concernant la monarchie absolue," *Storia Moderna.* Florence, 1955. Volume IV of *Relazioni del X congresso internazionale de scienzi storiche.*

Palmer, R. R. *Catholics and Unbelievers in 18th Century France.* Princeton, 1939.

Perey, Lucien. *Le Président Hénault et Madame du Deffand.* Paris, 1893.

Rocquain, Félix. *L'Esprit révolutionnaire avant la Révolution, 1715–1789.* Paris, 1878.

Scoville, Warren. *The Persecution of Huguenots and French Economic Development, 1680–1720.* Berkeley, 1960.

Sturgill, Claude. *Marshal Villars.* Lexington, Ky., 1966.

INDEX